READING and WRITING COMMUNITIES

May '93

For Mem,

Her ideas, enthusiasm and hard work inspire me. Her encouragement and appreciation support me.

With Thanks and love,

Julie

Reading and Writing Communities

CO-OPERATIVE LITERACY LEARNING IN THE CLASSROOM

SUSAN HILL and JOELIE HANCOCK

ELEANOR CURTAIN
PUBLISHING

First published in 1993
ELEANOR CURTAIN PUBLISHING
906 Malvern Road
Armadale 3143
Australia

Copyright © Susan Hill and Joelie Hancock 1993

All rights reserved.
Apart from any fair dealing for the purpose of study, research, criticism or review as permitted under the Copyright Act, no part of this book may be reproduced by any process without permission. Copyright owners may take legal action against a person who infringes their copyright through unauthorised copying. Inquiries should be directed to the publisher.

National Library of Australia
Cataloguing-in-publication data

Hill, Susan (Susan Elizabeth).
  Reading and writing communities.

  ISBN 1 875327 12 6

  1. Reading (Primary). 2. Language arts (Primary).
  I. Hancock, Joelie. II. Title.

372.6044

Production by Sylvana Scannapiego,
  Island Graphics
Edited by Ruth Siems
Designed by Sarn Potter
Cover design by David Constable
Cover photograph by Ray Stradwick
Typeset in 12/14pt Baskerville
  by Optima Typesetting and Design, Melbourne
Printed in Australia by Impact Printing

CONTENTS

Preface	vii
Introduction	1
1　A reading/writing community	5
2　Building cohesion	29
3　Co-operative learning and literacy	42
4　Setting and meeting goals: reading	62
5　Setting and meeting goals: writing	91
6　Reflections on building communities of readers and writers	122
References	130
Index	132

A community of readers and writers
is a group of people who value reading and writing
and who use it constantly for a wide range of purposes,
and where the members of the group
help each other to be successful.

PREFACE

Writing this book co-operatively took over two years. It is more intellectually demanding to work co-operatively, more challenging than working by yourself. We had to draw on our co-operative skills many times to pull ourselves out of debates where we circled around and could not move on. When working co-operatively, ideas have to be explained and made clear to the other person. Each person has to become familiar with and take on board the ideas of the other, while not losing the strength of their own point of view. Often our individual ideas had to be held at bay as we listened to understand the other's point of view. Then we added our ideas if we agreed or challenged and confronted if we did not. We were involved in critical debate throughout this book while we challenged each other's perspectives, conclusions and assumptions.

When we began, we agreed to take turns to write each chapter discussing our writing as we finished. We did not accept each other's half-formed ideas or partial understandings without seeking clarification. We critiqued, we asked each other for more evidence. We reshaped our own ideas and writing as a result.

We worked through all the ideas together and learned much about each other and how we both learn. We developed as individuals through this co-operative venture. We learned about each other's strengths, staying power and the need for fun and diversion when work became too serious and constant. We had many good times and frustrating times when we couldn't see the shape the book was taking at all. Its final shape is very different from our initial plans; the result of a joint struggle to make mutual sense of individual perspectives.

This book is a co-operative production. Many of these ideas are new; emerging from our observations, discussions with each other and the teachers, our reading and our separate and joint efforts.

We are grateful for the support of the staff and children at Taperoo Primary School, particularly the Principal Polly Eckert, Lyn Thompson and Sue Ryan. Lyn and Sue's commitment to children's development, their understanding of the curriculum and the learning process, their inventiveness and energy open up new directions for classroom teachers and make possible this book. Lyn Thompson wishes to acknowledge the following professional development programs: AWRITE, The Literacy Focus Schools Program and ESL in the Mainstream.

We also acknowledge the ideas and teaching of Rob Lees, Lorraine Leinert, Jane O'Loughlin, Judy Smith and Deirdre Travers. All are effective teachers whose innovative methods warrant documentation beyond this volume.

We are indebted to the University of South Australia for a research grant to document the building of communities of readers and writers and to Ray Stradwick who took many of the photographs.

We would like to acknowledge Eleanor Curtain, a fine publisher of teacher reference books, who continues to stimulate thinking within the educational community.

INTRODUCTION

Much of the story of human development must be written in the light of cultural influences in general and of the particular persons, practices and paraphernalia of one's culture. And chief among these, of course, in any complex culture will be such educational institutions as apprenticeships or formal schools.
Howard Gardner (p.39)

Literacy is a social event: language is learnt in communities. As new members seek to be accepted and to communicate with other members, they learn the vocabulary, purposes and patterns for communicating that are established in the community. They learn which ways of relating are acceptable and effective, which activities are valued, and what it is that they need to do to be fully accepted members of the community.

New communities are formed in classrooms every year. Each new class develops its own patterns of operating and ways of relating. The teacher has a major role in shaping which behaviours, which activities and which ways of interacting become the prevailing ones. The teacher's enthusiasm, provision of materials, and time allocation for particular activities generally reveal which activities have priority. The teacher who always finds plenty of time each day for story reading and children's writing demonstrates what she values. So too does the teacher who provides space for painting, different types of paper and brushes and plenty of room to display finished pictures. The teacher who rarely rushes students' exploration of maths material and reporting back of findings is also giving a clear message. Similarly, the teacher who spends considerable time in the first days of the year consistently making clear the sorts of behaviour that will be accepted in the class shows what she values. In each case the teacher is influencing the culture of the classroom community.

Teachers are not always in control of the patterns and values that are established in a class. Sometimes it is the students themselves who set the values and the prevailing ways of relating and of responding. On the other hand, teachers can be shocked to find the unintended influence they have had when they recognise their own gestures, tone of voice and phrases in a child playing 'teacher', or in a student's instructions to a younger student. Just as often, a teacher will realise that a group of students has learnt from a previous teacher to value a particular activity or way of behaving. This will be an advantage if the two teachers' beliefs about learning and relating are similar, but may require a lengthy program of relearning if, for instance, the former teacher required compliance and conformity while the new teacher aims for enquiry, risk-taking and individuality; if the former teacher focused on accurate word recognition within a particular set of books, while the new teacher values breadth of reading and interpretation.

There is no escaping the fact that the teacher has the power to shape what and how children will learn, and that teachers have the responsibility to establish a classroom community where children value learning and behave in ways that will enhance their own and each other's development.

This book documents the ways in which teachers are purposefully and strategically developing classroom communities whose members value and use reading and writing for their own purposes and pleasure. Where students come from homes where literacy is used for few purposes, and is seen as having a limited value, the teacher's role can be crucial in revealing that reading and writing have essential functions and are a source of pleasure. Where most members of the class community come from homes where literacy is already highly valued and constantly used, the teacher will still need to ensure that each child sees the relevance of reading and writing for his or her own satisfaction and purposes.

The development in classrooms of a sense of belonging and co-operation has become integral to learning the pleasures and uses of literacy; learning the behaviours and skills of helping and caring for each other is a high priority. Unless the members of a class are able to co-operate with each other (including the teacher) there is little chance of many of the students being able to enjoy and to have success with reading and writing. Where there is little co-operation, interruptions and distractions reduce the number and quality of positive learning experiences. Where there *is* co-operative learning, students

INTRODUCTION

are challenged by the different points of view and understandings of their peers, and learn to be critical of ideas rather than the people who have them. The quality and quantity of support that each child receives in becoming a successful reader and writer is increased.

The classrooms described in this book have teachers who recognise that co-operation and cohesion in the classroom are crucial to their students' success in literacy learning. They also believe that these characteristics are important for success in the other areas of the curriculum. Classroom cohesion and co-operation are valued and taught as part of every subject area. It is only where there is a shared culture built on co-operation and cohesion that all learners can be supported and challenged by each other, and all students can be successful.

Many of the ideas and teaching strategies presented here were generated at Taperoo Primary School where the two teachers most referred to in these pages were teaching. Taperoo is a forty-minute drive from Adelaide, past Port Adelaide. The school is classified as disadvantaged because of its high proportion of families who receive social security or live in difficult financial circumstances. One in seven students in the school is Aboriginal and a high proportion of parents were Indo-Chinese refugees. Other teachers referred to in this book work in a range of schools, both advantaged as well as those classified as socio-economically disadvantaged.

1
A Reading/ Writing Community

USING PRINT IN A READING/WRITING COMMUNITY

Literacy events that empower and strengthen a community do not always revolve around reading published texts. In Lyn Thompson's classroom the five-, six- and seven-year-old children learn to read and write while engaging in class meetings. Reading and writing, which follows critical debate and problem solving in class meetings, is an authentic way of demonstrating how the ideas and decisions made by the group of children can shape and create a democratic community. These children, like adults in the wider community, are using literacy to gain control and power over their lives. Writing and reading enables the children to record and remember class meeting decisions, reflect on these ideas, as well as read the appropriate procedures to run their own class meetings independently.

Reading is at work when the children take the role of chairperson and follow the chairperson's script during class meetings.

One Tuesday morning in spring, the children in Lyn Thompson's class were holding a class meeting. Natasha had taken the role of chairperson, and was halfway through the chairperson's script.
'Observer's report,' announces six-year-old Natasha.

Clinton stands up with the notes he has been making through the meeting and, with some quiet prompting from Julie, who is more experienced at reading and with the procedure, reads, 'Everyone was sitting flat. Six people were head nodding.'

'Feedback to the chairperson,' announces Natasha, and three hands go up to offer comments on how Natasha has conducted the meeting.

> **CHAIRPERSON'S SCRIPT**
>
> 1. 'Get ready.'
> 2. 'Good morning everyone.'
> 3. 'Has anyone got anything to show or say?'
> 4. 'Any comments or questions?'
> 5. 'Thank you . . .'
> 6. 'Observer's report.'
> 7. 'Feedback to the chairperson.'
> 8. 'Feedback from the chairperson.'
> 9. 'Bulletin.'
> 10. 'Agenda items.'
> 11. 'Time's up.'
> 12. 'The meeting is over.'

After three people have given their feedback, Natasha moves to the next item, 'Feedback from the chairperson.'

She reports, 'I liked that I didn't send anyone out,' then moves to the next item. 'The Bulletin,' she says.

Lyn Thompson, the teacher who has been sitting in the circle with her class, reads the daily school Bulletin: congratulations to two children who presented a poem at the school assembly, a brief report of the Year 7's visit to the local high school, details of the school fete to be held the next weekend.

'Agenda items,' introduces Natasha, and picks up a card on which children have written agenda items that they want the class to resolve. She says, 'Mary, will you elaborate?' because Mary has written her name beside the last recorded item. Mary reads out the dated item:

Mary says, 'Yesterday people were writing rude letters.'

AGENDA ITEMS

Date	Issue	Name
22.8.90	People putting stiky tap on their mouth	Sarah
22.8.90	Stepping on crayon	Mary
22.8.90	People biing notl won e/q the Ticha gos oat	Sharon
5.9.90	People writing rued Letters	Mary

A READING/WRITING COMMUNITY

The chairperson's script is written on a large chart, and can be referred to during the meeting.

Natasha addresses the whole class: 'Has anyone got any discussion about that?'

Class meetings are held whenever an item has been recorded on the agenda, generally once or twice a week. All members of the class take turns at being the chairperson, recorder and timer and are expected to participate in discussions. The responsibilities of each role have been demonstrated and listed earlier in the year. To help each chairperson there is a large chart with the twelve-itemed chairperson's script written on it; for the recorder there is a sheet of paper titled 'observation sheet', listing the behaviours to be recorded, attached to a clip board.

Natasha occasionally refers to the chairperson's script at her feet, but clearly needs no help in understanding the procedure or in performing her role. Clinton, who is in his first year at school and is still unsure of print, refers to his observation sheet to give his report. All the children are involved in finding a solution to a classroom concern identified and presented by one of the children. They all experience a procedure for jointly facing, exploring and resolving a social conflict. Mary has her problem from the day before resolved; in solving it the class revise their response to harassment, which has been introduced and practised over the last few months. The decision reached by the class is written on a card and pinned up with the many other decisions from previous meetings so that when concerns arise that have been dealt with before, the class have a ready reference.

READING AND WRITING COMMUNITIES

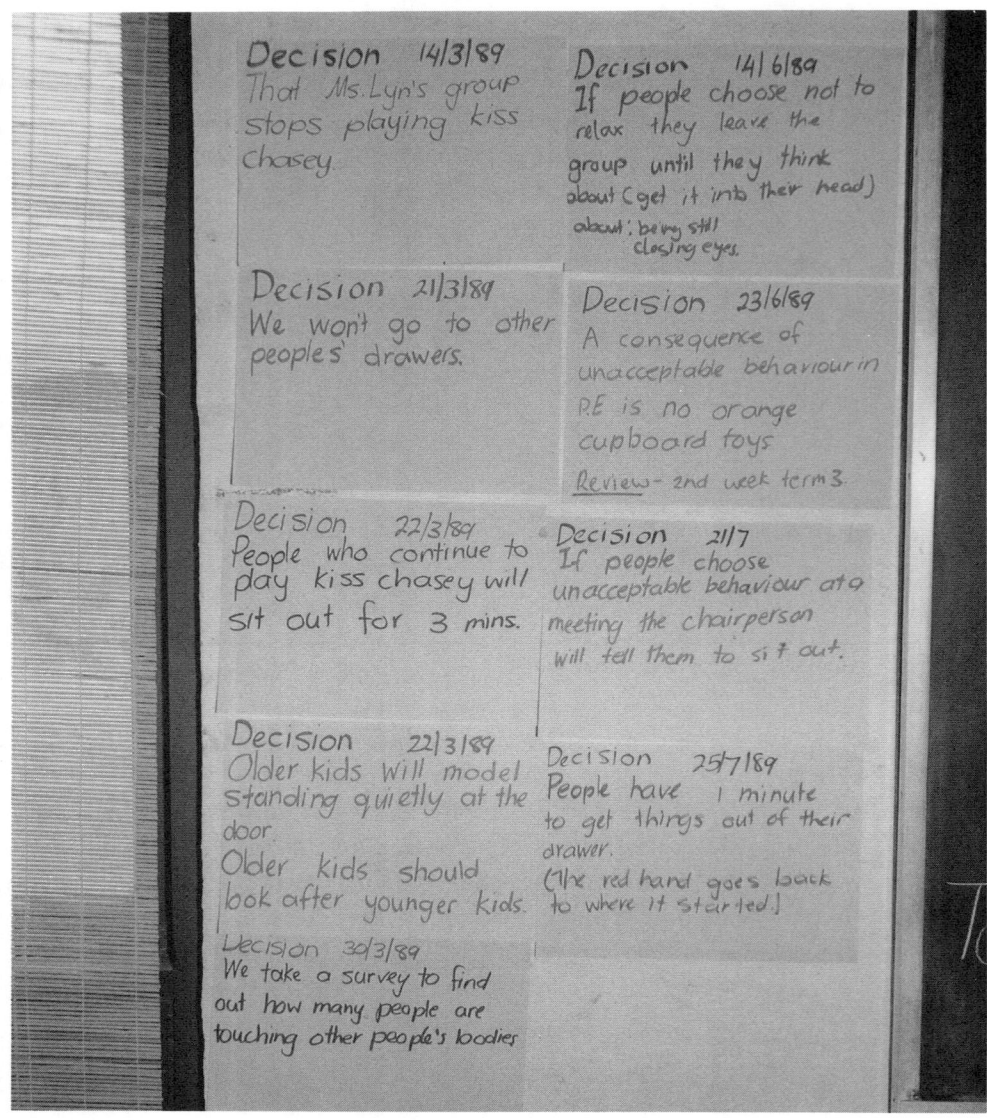

Class decisions are recorded and displayed for future reference.

STRUCTURING FOR USING PRINT

In this class, reading and writing are constantly being used to get things done. The students and the teacher write so that they can read what to do later, so that parents know what the children can do successfully at school, so they can let others know their ideas and opinions, so they can create a book for others to enjoy. They read so that they can check on ways of being successful in class activities, so that they can all join in with a favourite song, to share the stories they have written, so they know what they are meant to be doing, so that they can find out what others think and feel.

Lyn knows that a crucial part of being successful in our society is being able to read and write in a variety of ways. All the children in her class, from whatever background, bring experiences of reading and writing to school. Lyn helps them to appreciate the wide range of reading and writing that they do every day outside of school as well as in school, she shows them that these are valued, and she builds on these experiences to develop the children's confidence and skills with a wide range of text types and purposes.

Many children come from homes which are already small communities of literacy users: parents read books aloud to their children and selected pieces from newspapers and letters to other adults; an older brother or sister is seen curled up in a chair absorbed in a book or magazine, or writing at a table; family members leave notes for each other and add to the shopping list; they help each other with spelling and the right words for a notice; they regularly refer to the TV guide; and they find out who a letter is for by reading the envelope. In this class Lyn shows that she values these experiences, she introduces other purposes for reading and writing, teaches the children to be successful at reading and writing themselves, and develops the skills they need to be independent in learning and in working with others.

STRUCTURING FOR CO-OPERATION

From the first day at school the children are made aware that at school everyone has to work together so that everyone can learn. All members of the class are expected to contribute, have a turn, ask for help and offer help when they can see it is needed. In the class meeting reported above, Natasha was the chairperson, Clinton the observer and Cheryl the timekeeper because their turn had come up on the list attached to the chairperson's script chart. If it is their first time in a particular role there are ways of getting help without relying on the teacher.

It was Clinton's first turn as an observer so he was invited to choose a person to help him. He chose Mary who then sat beside him. She prompted him when he needed it but also knew how to do this without taking over. Clinton, although new in that role, had watched other children and knew without any reminding that he needed to fetch a clipboard, an observation sheet and a pencil, to watch and tick when he saw the three different behaviours listed, to use the help that Mary gave him, to stand up and 'read' his report when it was asked for. He has seen the pattern he is to follow, he accepts responsibility when it is his turn, he uses the literacy skills he has and he knows he can get the help he needs.

The children know what is expected from them because Lyn, their teacher, is very clear about the behaviour she expects from her children in every activity, and she makes these behaviours explicit in a number of ways. She also makes it clear that the children need to watch carefully to see how things are done in this class, and that they are expected to ask another child if they don't know what to do. For this is a class where the children learn to help each other to learn, and where the teacher sees her role as making this happen.

ABOUT THIS CLASSROOM COMMUNITY

Lyn Thomson's class is a composite Reception to Year 2 class with children aged between just 5 years to one child who is 8. Eleven are school beginners. Of the twenty-seven children in the class, fifteen live in traditional two-parent familiies, four live with their grandparents and seven live with either Mum or Dad. There are several different home cultures. Two of the children speak only Cambodian at home although they were born in Australia; also in the class are two Aboriginal children, a Vietnamese, a Fijian, a Turk and two Yugoslavian children.

The varied backgrounds of the children mean that they all come to school with different sets of behaviours for functioning successfully in their families. These skills, however, are not necessarily those needed for working co-operatively in a class with twenty-six peers and for learning new skills. Lyn knows that these children need to learn a wide range of social skills as well as skills for learning and problem solving if they are going to become successful in our society. And she is determined to begin that essential learning from their first day at school.

This book tells how Lyn and other teachers are building co-operative communities of readers and writers in their classrooms. For these teachers, a community of readers and writers is a group of people who value reading and writing and who use it constantly for a wide range of purposes, and where the members of the group help each other to be successful.

The rest of this chapter outlines a number of strategies for creating such a community.

A WIDE RANGE OF TEXTS AND PURPOSES THROUGHOUT THE SCHOOL

At Taperoo, as in many other primary schools, there is print wherever you look. There are signs and posters that you will see in most schools: telling visitors and children which way to go, captions on children's art, posters about authors, lists of words that the children have contributed as the teacher wrote, poems in large type that the children have composed. But there is something distinctive about the texts displayed: most of them are continually referred to by the children and teachers. They are there to be used, not merely to be looked at or to decorate the walls.

There are a number of Y charts. These serve several purposes and are a good example of how writing and reading and texts are used for a variety of purposes. Y charts:

- provide a powerful vocabulary
- provide a structure for examining an issue or behaviour
- make explicit a range of behaviours
- provide depth to discussion on behaviour or an issue
- provide the tools for children to be explicit and critical
- put children in touch with their feelings and their behaviour
- extend their emotional range (not just 'sad' or 'happy')
- help confront children with the effect they have on others
- legitimise and encourage discussion of feelings
- are used for a variety of purposes

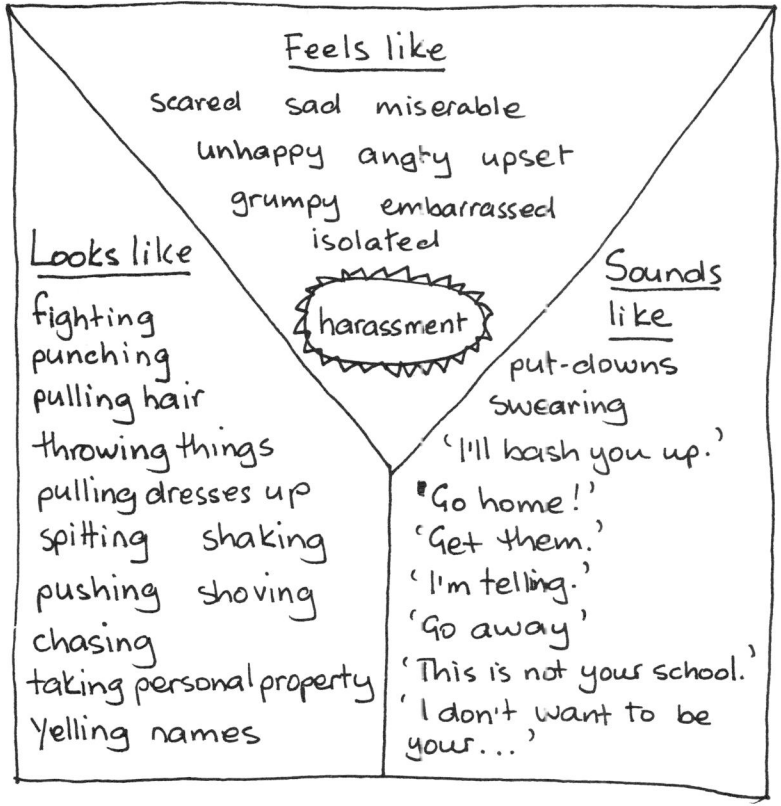

This chart on harassment is referred to again and again. It was developed to provide vocabulary to express feelings and behaviour after some conflict in the playground. The Y chart was used to develop strategies to deal with harassment.

Lyn had the class construct a Y chart on herself as part of a unit on similarities and differences in people and to demonstrate construction of a Y chart on a person, as opposed to the charts on behaviour that they were already familiar with.

Lyn demonstrates the construction of a Y chart on a person.

The children later referred back to this chart to make a Y chart on themselves, to gain a deeper awareness of the different dimensions of themselves and others — what they do, what they look like, say and feel like — and a fuller understanding of what is involved in constructing a Y chart.

These charts about themselves were later used to prepare the big book on the class in which each child had a page with a photograph of themselves and a description. This book was frequently in demand when the children had free choice with reading. Generally two or three children would read it together.

The most used chart in the class is the list of criteria for a happy day. It was developed early in the year when the class were focusing on what each of them needed to do to have a successful and happy day. The children and Lyn refer to the ten items on this chart as 'the

Did you have a good day?

Criteria

1. feeling happy
2. having fun
3. staying on task
4. finishing work on time
5. listening
6. teacher says terrific
7. people working
8. following instructions
9. keep the room tidy
10. talking quietly

criteria'. The class use the criteria to evaluate their behaviour after an art class, being with a relieving teacher, lining up, walking to the toilet. Self-assessment of behaviour in terms of the criteria occurs several times a week.

There are a number of role statements around the room. Lyn has written them, with help from the class, after the children have observed and discussed what the various roles look like, sound like and feel like. They refer to these role descriptions when preparing for the roles and afterwards when evaluating their own behaviour.

Another class activity that entails another set of charts is the class meeting. A meeting is called whenever a child has written up a problem they want discussed. The charts used are a T chart on a class meeting, a roster for the different roles in a meeting, the script for the chairperson, the agenda where the problem has been recorded, a recording sheet for the observer, and a decision notice that is attached to the wall with all class decisions.

Texts are created to record decisions, make roles explicit and clarify the democratic processes that underpin the classroom community.

Chairperson's script.

A READING/WRITING COMMUNITY

Every class topic generates its own set of charts, with the particular vocabulary and forms that relate to that topic. The charts are taped to the wall for easy reference during the topic.

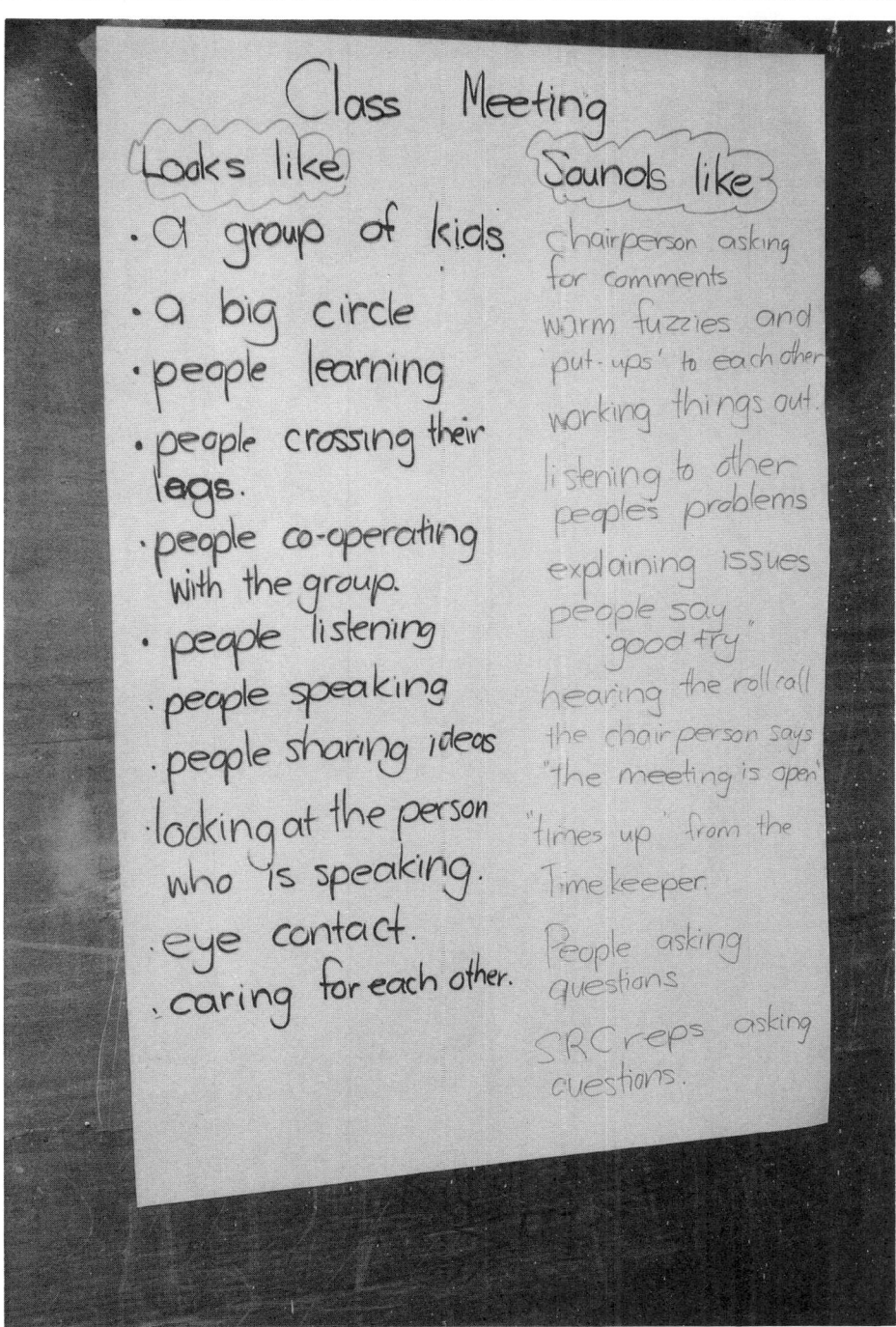

T chart on class meetings.

Roster for meeting roles.

A READING/WRITING COMMUNITY

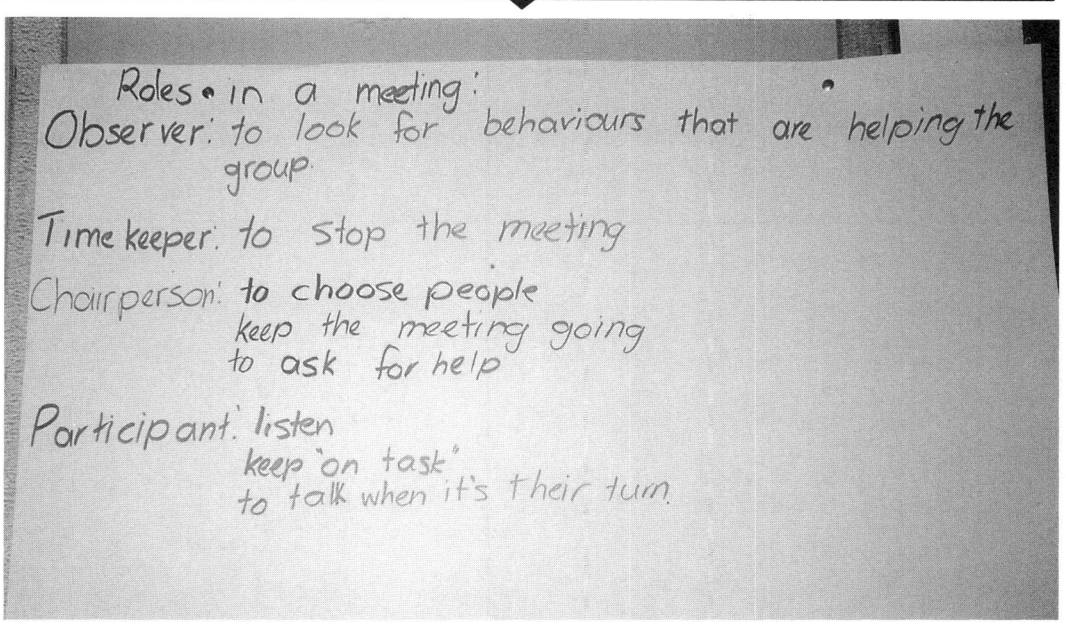

List of meeting roles.

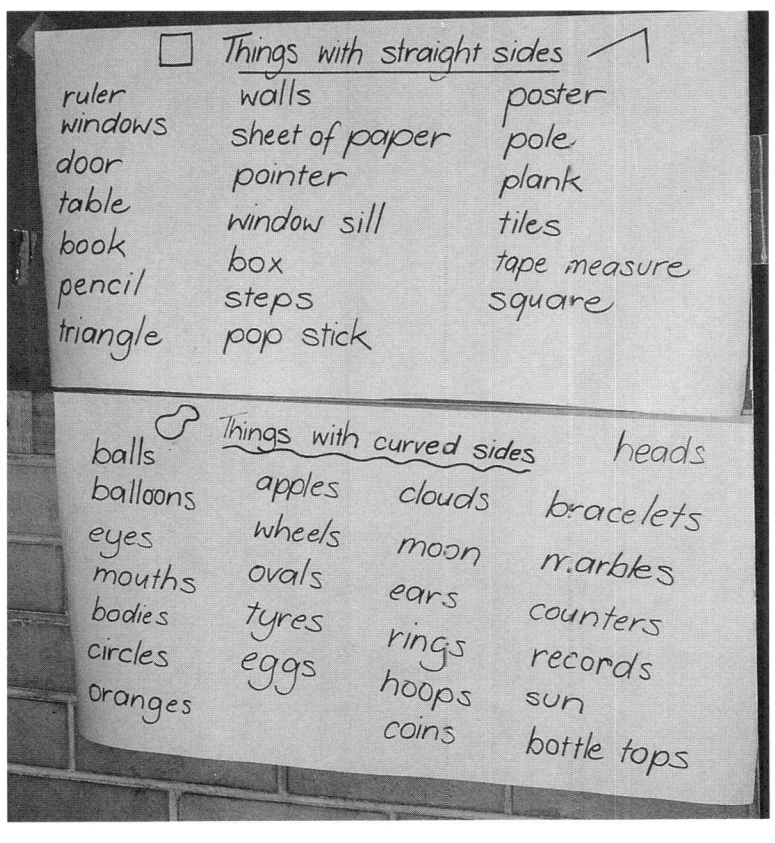

Each class topic generates its own set of charts.

One topic that involved much exploration and helped the children to realise that the community of readers was active at home as well as at school, was a survey of the types of things read at home.

And there are other charts that help with the day-to-day classroom organisation.

'When you have finished writing.'

Working in groups.

READING AND WRITING COMMUNITIES

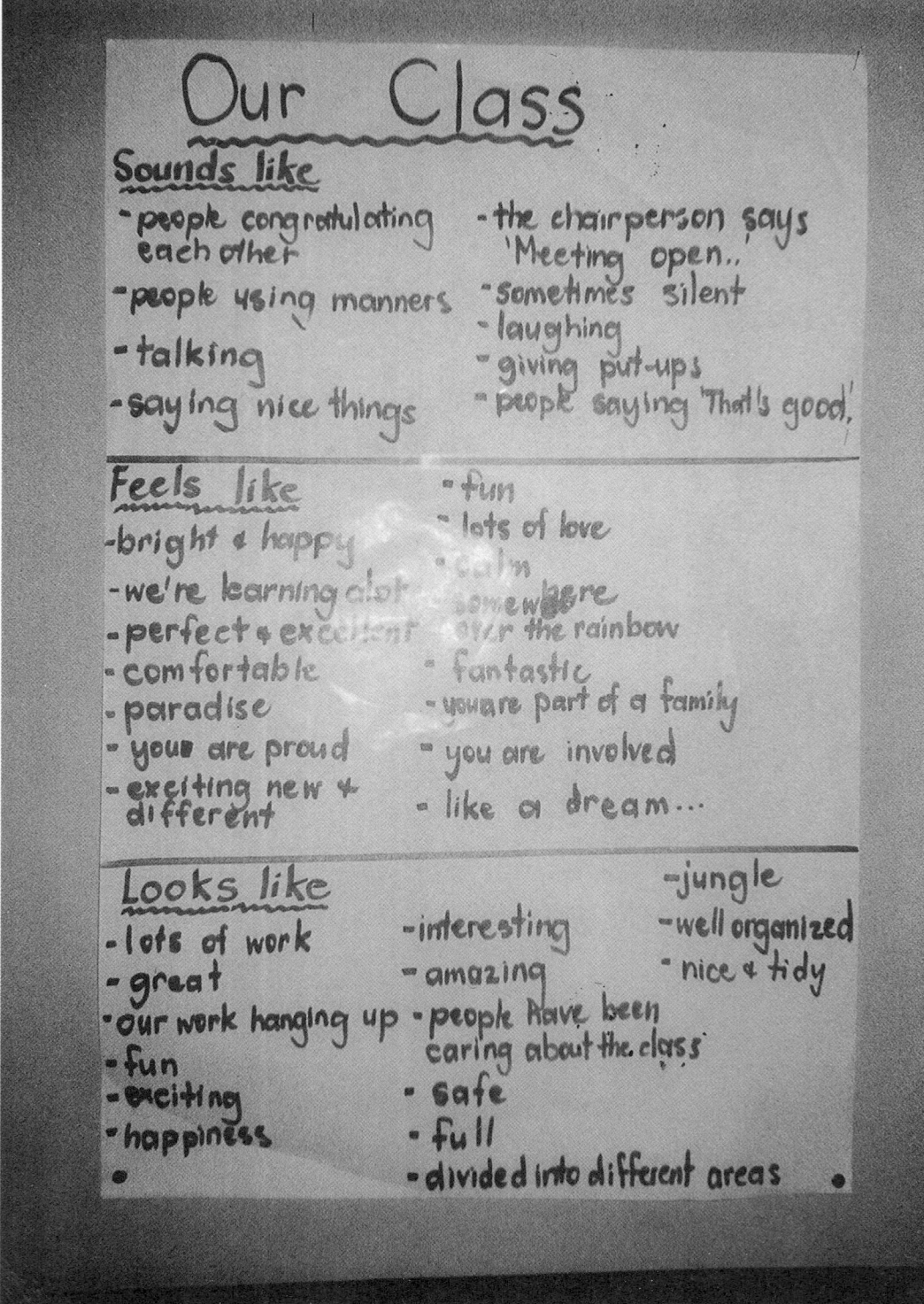

T chart on the class.

Activity wheel.

Then there is the reading for the joy of it: the large charts of songs, raps and rhymes that the children share at least once every day. Lyn has searched out and tested the rhymes over her years of teaching to compile a collection that she knows these children will enjoy.

THE SCHOOL AS A LITERACY COMMUNITY

It is not only in classrooms that the children at Taperoo experience useful and enjoyable written texts. The staff have worked out their priorities for the students and make clear by what is displayed around the school and by their own behaviour that reading and writing are highly valued. Students see print as a means of sharing information, as a way to make things happen, and as a source of pleasure.

PRINT TO SHARE INFORMATION AROUND THE SCHOOL

Around the school, at appropriate places, there are charts that record negotiated school beliefs and goals, make achievements of particular students known to the whole school community and provide information about sporting teams and their achievements.

Negotiated school beliefs are displayed around the school.

A READING/WRITING COMMUNITY

Students see print as a way of sharing information.

Teachers understand that most of the information coming to them from the principal is relevant to the children and helps them to feel responsible members of the whole school community. The weekly bulletin written by the principal is therefore read and discussed with the children in each class. The bulletin contains information about staff members, visitors to the school, staff meetings and conferences, approaching excursions and sporting events, assembly plans and other information that affects the whole school community.

Teachers also believe that if children and parents are provided with specific and regular written information on the children's achievements, both the children and the parents can understand what the school is trying to achieve and play a more active part in the learning. Written feedback comes in many forms: in 'read all about it' books, with sections on the child's own goals and achievements, in certificates recognising a child's achievements, and in the written report that goes home each term.

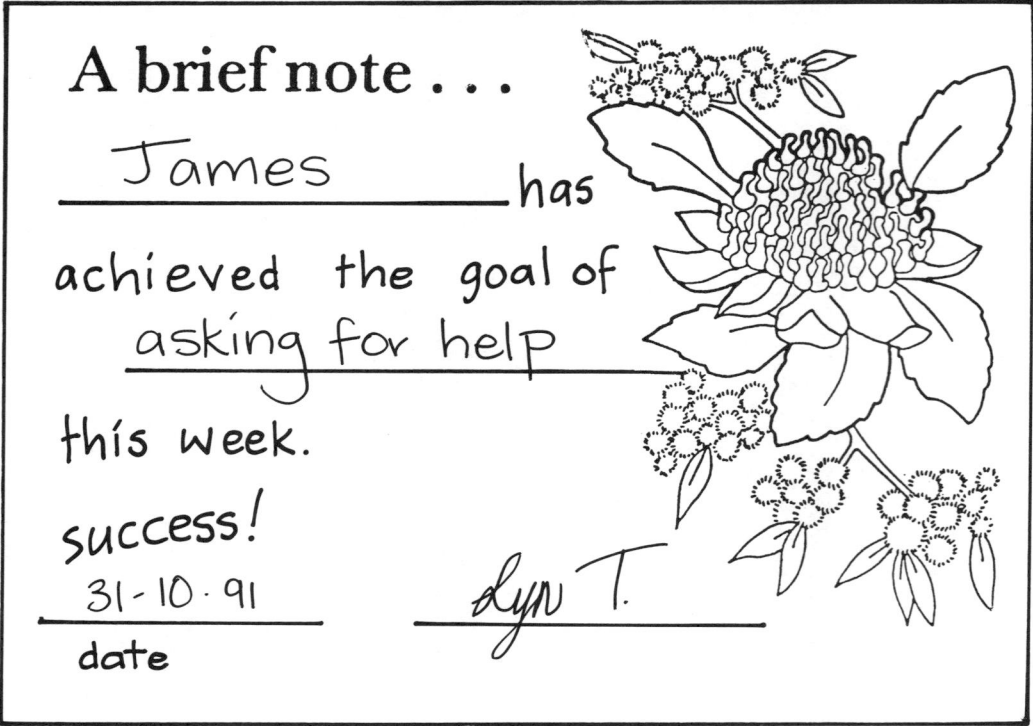

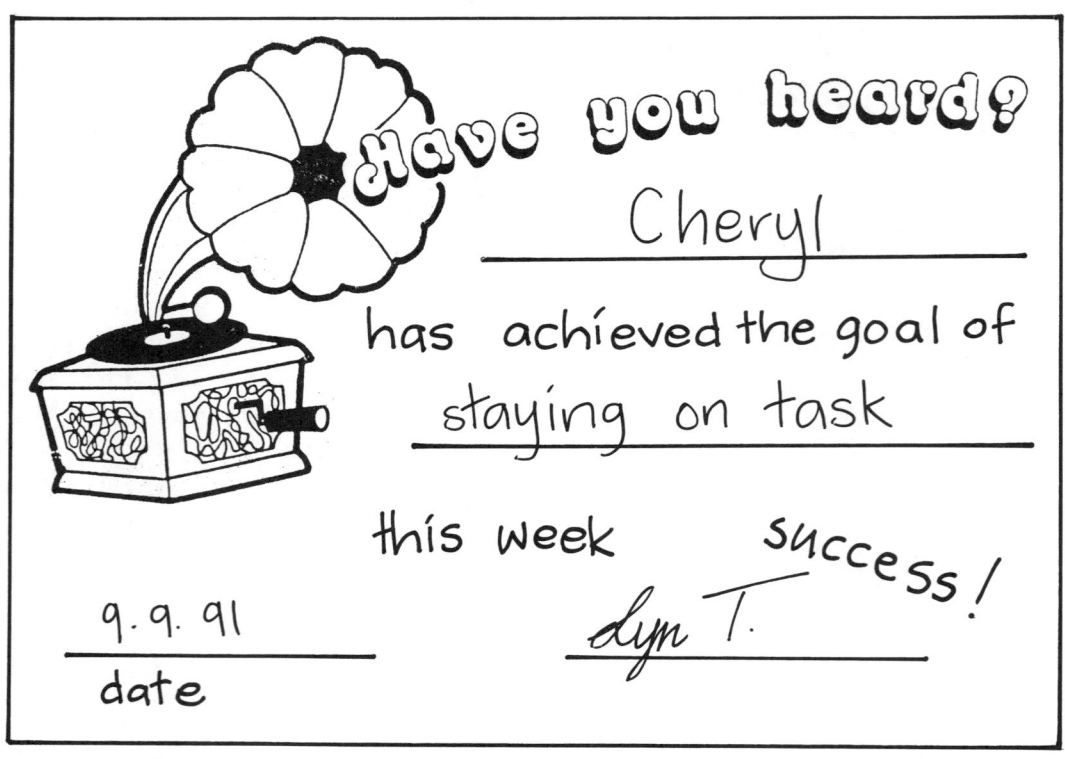

A READING/WRITING COMMUNITY

Sarah H

You were busy in Activity time today! Making a play

Lyn 17/5

Please sign, date, and comment (if you wish) after reading with your child

Date	Name of Book	Sign / Date	Listener's Comment	Lyn's Comment
13/9	Bertie & the bear			had trouble with names
5/9	Riddles	20/9	Read this book 4 times He thouroughly enjoyed testing everyone in our house Read well	yes!
20/9	Caps for sale	21/9	Didn't read to me last night	We've got the same favorite part
10/10	Fish stay	10/10		
12/10	Mogs Mumps	12/10	Had problems with long words unable to say catastrope let alone	read it
14/10	Meg's Eggs	13/10	Had trouble with some words	- he appears keen - and keeps trying
15/10	Meg at Sea	14/10	Read this book with minimum problems	great!
17/10	Mag at the zoo			

READING AND WRITING COMMUNITIES

PRINT AS A WAY TO MAKE THINGS HAPPEN

In various places around the school, a visitor will come across posters that set out clearly and specifically what is expected in various places and for particular activities.

Our class counsellors are

Shanadene, Lana and Aaron

Their role is

- to be here if needed
- to help solve problems
- to listen
- to mediate
- to hear both sides of the story
- to give advice
  (e.g. to Ms Giles)

They are available

- before school
- after school
- lunch time
- recess time

Class mediator

Check that those involved want to resolve their problems

Check that they are happy for you to be the mediator

Try to find some commonground, some points of agreement.

Encourage them to think of several possible solutions before selecting one to act on.

A READING/WRITING COMMUNITY

```
                        MY PLAN         Date: _____
   Name: _____
   What did you do?

   What rule did you break?

   Do you want to work out a way to follow the rules and be part of the
   class again?

   What is your plan to follow the rules?

   When will we check on your plan?


   Signed: _____
```

Like the posters in Lyn Thomson's class, these written procedures and statements are the culmination of demonstrations, discussion and negotiation of what should be included.

PRINT AS A SOURCE OF PLEASURE

Programming silent reading across the school at the same time every day has helped all students in many schools to realise that adults and children of all ages can be lost in a book. Having the whole school fall silent after lunch with five-year-olds, teacher aids, secretary and principal all reading quietly is a powerful way of showing what the school values.

Regular partner reading, where cross-age partners from two different classes choose a book together, read it together and talk about it, has also widened students' appreciation of what others like and respond to. What Lyn valued most from the regular partner reading sessions her R to 2 class had with a Year 5 class was the opportunity for the younger children to see what more able readers do when they read, and to see them enjoying reading.

The teacher is a powerful model of the pleasures of reading and Lyn, the other teachers, the principal and the teacher librarian at Taperoo make sure that they make the time to demonstrate their passion for reading, for particular books and for favourite authors. Their passion is evident, not just in the interest they show in what the children read, but also in their eagerness to get back to a book being read to the class, their obvious engagement in the stories they share, their pleasure in discussing a book or an author with the children, and their absorption in reading during silent reading time.

Every day throughout the school the children at Taperoo see print used to achieve a range of purposes. They see others writing to record what has happened and they experience the many ways that writing is returned to for confirmation of past events and for information. They learn that for pleasure and to get things done, reading and writing are powerful skills.

2

BUILDING COHESION

◆

CLASSROOMS HAVE THEIR OWN CULTURE

Sam has arrived late at school. He looks around the room at what the children are doing. It is activity time, and a group at a table are making patterns with stamps, another group are 'playing school' at a large blackboard, on the floor another group construct hats with stiff coloured paper, there are pairs and single children reading books, a group around Lyn, reading, and another group pasting at a table. Sam goes directly to Clinton at the stamping table and asks, 'Clinton, what are we meant to be doing?' Clinton points to the activity wheel which shows today's activity for each group of children, with the names of all the children listed. He says he can't read it but, 'You could ask Panat.' This Sam does, but Panat can't read either. He directs Sam to Michael, who Panat knows is able to read the wheel. Michael stops what he is doing and goes with Sam to the activity wheel where, after some searching, they find Sam's name and his activity for the day.

Five-year-old Sam arrived at Taperoo in third term and has been there for five weeks. On his first day he stood vaguely looking at what was going on in the room. From this first day he has been expected to be a responsible, fully participating member of the group. Lyn told him in that first ten minutes, 'In this class, if you are not sure what to do, ask someone,' and throughout that first day and every other day Lyn and other members of the class have spelt out or demonstrated the behaviour that is expected. Lyn is explicit about what is required:

In this class we say 'No thank you' if we don't want a turn.

James spoke clearly so we could hear him.

Stop everyone, look at Helen's work. She has set it out so that we can follow it easily.

Sam did not have to go across the circle to find a space, he asked someone to move along.

Panat do you want something? If you tell me what you want then I can help you.

Only people who have paper underneath can use the stamps.

Rebecca waited until she could face the circle so that we could hear her.

Only people who can speak clearly can have a turn.

I can see Mary giving eye contact.

Marcus is nodding and showing that he's listening.

Sarah's moved over so that Christopher can sit down.

That's a statement that shows you were really on task.

With statements such as these Lyn continually reflects the behaviours that are part of this class's culture. By stating the successful behaviour that she sees she is letting some children know that they are behaving appropriately and reminding others what the expected behaviours are. The behaviour and the vocabulary that defines it help to establish the culture of the classroom, the culture that all members of the class are helped to become a part of.

It wasn't easy for Sam to adjust to the class culture. In his first weeks he preferred to look down, shake his head and say nothing when it was his turn to share in the circle. His way of coping was to stay uninvolved, to stand and watch and hope that he wouldn't be noticed. His way of relating and gaining attention was to annoy people, nudging them hard, taking their things. Lyn gently persisted, making uncooperative behaviour less and less desirable, and co-operative behaviour like joining in and helping others easier and more attractive. After five weeks Sam is now a fully participating member of that community — not always wanting to conform with its patterns, but more willing to belong and much more skilled in being a supportive member.

BUILDING A COHESIVE CULTURE

Group cohesion is the bond between group members that unites them in working towards common goals. Group cohesion comes from having a shared culture: similar goals, common ways of doing things, shared vocabulary and phrases, and a basic acceptance of the differences within the group. A shared culture allows the children to get on with the tasks of the classroom. Their attention is not diverted by concerns about fitting in or gaining recognition. They feel they belong, safe to focus on the challenges planned for their learning.

Lyn is clear about her role in establishing a classroom culture. From the first day of the school year she lays the foundations of belonging by negotiating the class goals, introducing the vocabulary of learning and working together, and making clear the ways of behaving that will enable all class members, including herself, to operate successfully in the class.

> *My role is to make clear what the culture is here and where we're going as a class. From the beginning of the year I am clear about many of the behaviours that I want, such as speaking clearly, acknowledging your partner, asking for help, staying on task. But many of the classroom patterns and rules emerge as the need arises and the class have a chance to discuss and make decisions about them.*
>
> *My role is to be very clear about the behaviours that we are aiming for. Making things explicit is basic to the way I work.*

Cohesion is a sense of belonging, and is necessary if children are to work co-operatively. At the same time, working co-operatively builds cohesion. This chapter describes how Lyn and other teachers develop this sense of belonging in their classrooms, through

- developing a sense that the class is special
- establishing successful behaviour
- establishing a common language
- developing responsibility
- developing co-operation

WE ARE SPECIAL

Lyn builds the community slowly. She uses sharing circles to tell the children about herself and for them to tell about themselves. At this stage sentence starters such as 'I'm Lyn and I'm good at . . .' and 'At home I like to . . .' are helpful. These opportunities to know what is special about each class member help to define the group and acknowledge strengths as well as differences of the members of the group.

At the beginning of the year a lot of time is given to songs, raps and rhymes. Lyn's eleven years in priority project schools have given her a keen eye and ear for the rhymes that appeal to the children, although she always checks them out with each class and is prepared to discard any that are sexist or racist or that do not keep the children's

READING AND WRITING COMMUNITIES

Lyn uses sharing circles to find what is special about each class member.

interest. She knows that the children most enjoy rhymes with a definite rhythm, repetition and humour, as well as something distinctive such as increasing pace, decreasing volume, syncopated beats or unusual actions. Several times a day the children join in for at least six rhymes, with great enthusiasm, bobbing to the beat, clicking their fingers, swaying and singing. The children who cannot read the words soon pick them up through repetition, and all of them can do the actions and move to the rhythms. The emphasis is always on enjoyment and joining in.

As the year progresses these rhymes continue to provide a time to relax and have fun — at least once every day. The class gradually builds a repertoire of over thirty rhymes, as well as the sense of being united and totally engaged in an enjoyable activity.

Other literature provides the class with a shared language, characters they all know, experiences they can share, and, just as important, times when they feel strong emotions together. Stories have always proved worthwhile, not only to extend the children's language and knowledge of the world, but to provide a core of shared pleasurable experiences. Lyn reads stories to her class at least three times a day. She reads with enthusiasm, showing deep involvement with the stories, and expressing her own reactions, questions and predictions. The children are also encouraged to respond to the stories. At the end of a story as many as twelve children will put up their hands to give a comment about

BUILDING COHESION

the part they liked, similarities they have noticed in their lives or w. other stories, patterns seen in the text. This sharing of reactions another way that the children develop bonds with each other.

ESTABLISHING SUCCESSFUL BEHAVIOURS

Lyn begins to create an awareness of the behaviour that is expected in the class by confirming the successful behaviours that the children bring to school, and by being a clear model of the behaviours that she knows to be most effective for co-operation and effective communication. Well before planning a lesson where these behaviours are made explicit, Lyn demonstrates good communication with eye contact, nodding, puzzled looks when not understanding, and expressions of interest, and she gives recognition to the behaviours that are valued with comments such as 'James is sitting quietly and giving eye contact' and 'Susan has decided to write a letter.'

Lyn takes every opportunity to state the approved behaviours as they occur, so that the children are sure of what is expected in the class. Drawing attention to good work, thanking children for co-operative behaviour, and asking for help herself are some of the other incidental ways that she signals the norms of appreciating and relying on each other.

Lyn is careful to give the children time and space to come to terms with the new classroom setting and behaviour patterns. She constantly observes the children to see which behaviours need developing and which children need more support, feedback and time, and to help her plan class activities and expectations to match the children's readiness to concentrate and consider others.

There are a number of behaviours that Lyn knows are basic if her students are to function well as a co-operative, learning community.

- For communicating:
    look at the speaker
    listen silently
    nod head
    smile
    no put-downs
    take turns
    ask if you don't understand

- In the class circle:
    speak to the centre of the circle
    empty hands
    hands in laps
    keep things to share behind your back
    speak clearly

sit flat
make room for others

- Paired or individual work:
    keep on task
    complete set task
    knee to knee
    watch or ask others if not sure what to do
    monitor your own behaviour

These behaviours are not established overnight. They take careful and deliberate planning, beginning with the teacher's own modelling of them and acknowledging these behaviours when the children show them.

SIX STRATEGIES FOR ESTABLISHING EXPECTED BEHAVIOUR

In Lyn's class there are six general strategies she uses to clarify and reinforce the behaviours that are acceptable in this classoom culture. Each of the six strategies builds on the others.

- class rules and class meeting decisions
- successful behaviours
- the three-step process: make it explicit, practice and feedback[*]
- self-evaluation circle
- trust blocks
- goal setting

- **Class rules** are developed at the beginning of the year and adapted as the year progresses. Lyn developed the list of rules by having the children consider what happens on days when everyone is happy.

Did you have a happy day?

1. Feeling happy
2. Having fun
3. Staying on task
4. Finishing work on time
5. Teacher says 'Good work' 'Terrific' 'That's good'
6. Listening
7. People working
8. Following instructions
9. Keeping the room tidy
10. Talking quietly

[*]Johnson and Johnson (1990)

The list of behaviours became the 'Criteria for a happy day' and is regularly used to assess the day.

To refine the behaviours that make the classroom a happy and working environment, the class meetings allow the children to raise and resolve conflicts or problems that they notice.

- **'Successful behaviours'** is the term for the specific behaviours that are identified, listed and practised throughout the day. The class has a 'successful behaviours book' in which are listed (one list on each page) the specific behaviours that are effective for activities such as listening, paired reading, partner talks, relaxation, activity time.

- **The three-step process**: (1) make it explicit, (2) practice and (3) feedback, is a cyclical process that Lyn is committed to for establishing the successful behaviours that are needed for effective learning. The first step is to make visible, to articulate and to write down the particular behaviours that are effective for a particular activity. The class forms a circle around children who are good models for the activity and the children describe the behaviour they see. Lyn writes down what they describe. For partner reading she wrote in the successful behaviours book:

Partner reading

1. Read quietly
2. Helping
   - tell them the word
   - sound or spell
3. Reading all of the book
4. Keep on task
5. Listen to your partner

Next time the class has partner reading the successful behaviours are revised by reference to this list and by Lyn reporting incidentally, and at the the end of the session, the behaviours listed that she could see. The children occasionally evaluate their own partner reading behaviour, with each child in the class circle reporting which of the listed behaviours he or she exhibited during that particular session.

Partner reading is one of the many activities for which successful behaviours can be established.

- **Self-evaluation circles**, described above for partner reading, are a regular feature of Lyn's class. Most often the behaviours focused on for evaluation are those listed for a happy day. Lyn asks each child, 'Did you meet the criteria?' They answer 'Yes' or 'No'. If no, the child will often state which criteria was not met: 'No I didn't stay on task.' Lyn encourages the children to set goals for their class behaviour based on these evaluations.
- **Trust blocks** were introduced to provide an incentive for the whole class to take responsibility for their own and each other's behaviour. The trust block is a rectangular card divided into five squares, one for each letter in the word *TRUST*. When every member of the class in an evaluation circle says that they have met the criteria, the class receives a letter in one of the boxes. When the whole card is filled (the word *TRUST* has been completed), the class chooses how they want to celebrate — an extra turn in the gym, a visit to the local kindergarten, a picnic at a nearby park.
- **Goals** are formally set in two ways: as part of the term plan for a particular subject area, or fortnightly when each class member states some particular behaviour that they want to improve. Each term, for instance, the class select six to eight types of writing that each member will attempt during that term. The chosen types are listed

on a sheet that is pasted into each student's writing book and as each type is tried it is marked off. The individual behaviour goals are stated by each child, recorded and posted on the wall for checking in a fortnight's time. An achievement certificate is given to each child who has achieved their goal.

Goals

Tanya: eye contact

Sean: sit with new people

Micheal: follow instructions

Gemma: play with new people

Elizabeth: follow instruction

Simon: talk in circle time

Cheryl: follow instruction

Anton: talk quietly while working

Phanat: be on time

Rebecca: sit with new people

Aliscia: finish work on time

Clinton: keep on task

A COMMON LANGUAGE

If children are going to make fine distinctions in behaviour and communicate with precision, they need to hear and use exact language. Lyn believes that the language of the mainstream culture needs to become available to all children, and it is only in school that many children will have access to the mainstream language. For this reason Lyn never speaks down to her class. The children soon learn to respond to and use terms such as *agenda, elaborate, feedback, information, item, more equitable, harassment, helpful strategy,* and make distinction between terms such as *recount/report/record, journal/diary, comment/opinion/question, prediction/estimate/summary.*

Lyn believes, 'If you give children soft options you make life hard for them.'

INDIVIDUAL AND GROUP RESPONSIBILITY

The fourth component of building cohesion in a class is member responsibility. The teacher explains who is responsible for what, and that the children have responsibility for their own behaviour as well as for the successful functioning of the whole class.

In practice this means each child first makes sure they are meeting their own responsibilities. The behaviours required for this are those included as the criteria for a happy day: staying on task, finishing work on time, following instructions, talking quietly and keeping the room tidy.

Since many of the classroom learning tasks and activities are co-operative, completing these tasks requires working successfully with other members of the class. The successful behaviours for communicating, paired work and circle time, are each child's responsibility to maintain. Lyn watches and knows her children well, and varies her expectations and support. She will continually remind some children of the behaviours that they should be focusing on, often by referring to another child's positive behaviour,

Mary has tidied up her area and is sitting quietly in the circle.

And sometimes by stating the behaviours:

In the circle we put our things to show behind us.
When people are sitting in the circle and are comfortable we can go on.
We can only go on when the area is tidy.

As the children become familiar with their responsibilities, more of the onus is placed with the child:

What are you doing David?
What are you meant to be doing Simon?

Lyn often refers to the children's rights and responsibilities.

You have a right to be a group member. But if you are a group member you have responsibilities, and one of these is that you make a space for other people.

One of the rights that is accepted in the class is the right to have a turn at every role and activity. Along with that right is the right to have help if you need it. The corollary of this is that you also have responsibility to provide help when it is needed. Lyn makes these rights and responsibilities clear.

Perhaps more difficult than balancing these rights and responsibilities is the balancing of individual and group responsibilities. The balance of these is often confusing to some children, particularly those who have little confidence in their own judgement. But gradually they learn that their first priority as a group member and as an individual is to be sure that they themselves are behaving appropriately and then, if they can see that they might contribute to the group or help another member, they should.

Michael is finishing some maths work during Activity Time. He is busy creating a maths pattern with stamps along with three other children who did not complete this activity the day before. Sean has been reading to Lyn and together they have concluded that he should get some more practice in reading his book by finding a partner who can help him by reading with him. Sean knows that Michael is a willing helper, so asks him if he will read with him. Michael agrees to help and Sean sits next to Michael and reads, every now and then asking Michael to help him with a particular word. Michael does not look comfortable helping; he continues to make an effort to continue with the stamp pattern that he knows he is meant to be focusing on. Later when Lyn confronts Michael about why he hasn't finished his maths she knows that he has had his attention diverted by helping someone else. He explains that he was helping Sean, but does know what he should have chosen to do.

Lyn: What was was your first responsibility?

Michael: To finish my maths.

Lyn: You should have said to Sean, 'I'm sorry I can't read with you because I have to finish my maths'.

Lyn knows that all children can be successful. From whatever point they begin, they can make progress. It is this progress and achievement rather than the differences in starting points that Lyn focuses on in her class. She helps each child to feel successful, to know what successful behaviour is and so recognise when they have achieved it. From this knowledge the children can then realistically set goals and evaluate their achievements.

COHESION AND TRUST

In classrooms where there is no trust, students will avoid taking risks. They will not attempt to answer questions unless they are sure of the answers; they will not offer suggestions in case of ridicule; and they will often conceal their true interests and capabilities if they are not seen to be in line with the dominant group in the class.

This counterculture of the peer group which can drastically interfere with classroom learning is well known to upper primary teachers. At this level there is considerable peer pressure not to conform to adult expectations, not to appear more able than others, and not to take the risk of trying something new in case of failure or meeting peer disapproval. Appropriate shared goals, trust built from knowledge that the other students and the teacher will accept and support their efforts, and acceptance of differences are the three essentials of a class where all its members learn effectively and co-operatively.

Lyn uses a number of strategies to develop cohesion.

Without class cohesion students are continually distracted from their learning by members who have other priorities. Instead of wanting to achieve the negotiated class goals, such as completing a given task, some students have an investment in gaining attention, diverting commitment away from approved tasks and reducing the trust among class members.

Like Lyn, Rob Lees, a junior primary teacher of many years, believes that in the early years of school the lack of trust that is most likely to interfere with children's learning is their lack of trust in themselves. Rob, in teaching a Reception to Year 1 class at Ascot Park Primary School, sets out to create a classroom where the children can focus on their learning and work co-operatively with each other. At the beginning of the year he sees his class as full of individuals with their own separate intentions and behaviours. In such a class the children who do not want to or do not know how to fit in make it difficult for all the class members to work productively.

Many of the children believe they cannot be successful and have learnt a pattern of saying 'I can't' to themselves and to adults. They gain satisfaction through playing up, and avoid responsibility by daydreaming and being 'cute'.

In order to establish cohesion in his class of individuals Rob finds that he must first focus on achieving two preliminary goals. First, all the children must experience success and learn to recognise and appreciate their own successes. Second, they must learn appropriate class behaviour so they can operate as responsible learners. They must learn not to disturb others, to listen to directions and carry them out, and to independently engage with approved tasks without disturbing or being interrupted by others. It is only when children can engage independently with tasks that they can become effective learners in the classroom.

Rob works consistently at making explicit the behaviours that are required, acknowledging when those behaviours are evident, and building a cohesive community through experiences that are enjoyed together, and where the clear expectation is to help each other.

3
Co-operative Learning and Literacy

♦

Before introducing her class to co-operative learning Lyn Thompson observed that pairs of children in reading and writing activities worked quite effortlessly with each other until the task or activity became difficult, and then conflict led to disintegration of the partnership. Once disagreements occurred children withdrew, got angry and decided that person was 'not my friend'. Much of Lyn's time was then spent as peacemaker.

Two years ago, when Lyn asked the class to choose a partner, she saw the articulate children quickly choose each other, Aboriginal children choose each other, and boys choose boys. There were always two or three children not chosen at all until the bitter end when Lyn intervened. Lyn remembers that if a circle was formed for class discussion sometimes one or two rejected children walked round and round the circle trying to find a space to sit — because no one made a space for them. It seemed to be the case of the 'rich getting richer' and this did not fit with Lyn's beliefs about social justice or children learning from positive role models.

Lyn recalled that when children gave each other feedback about their writing it was rarely positive, but focused on the what was wrong rather than its strengths. The children were learning to not take each other seriously. Before Lyn introduced co-operative learning the children put each other down, boys put down girls and the more articulate children scored points at the expense of others with less well developed skills.

Lyn has spent the last two years developing her ideas about building a cohesive, co-operative classroom. She is still developing and changing because co-operative learning, with its framework of co-operative skills and co-operative structures, provides endless possibilities for improving literacy learning.

Many of the co-operative skills for working together are communication skills like turn-taking, one person speaks, avoiding put-downs, listening and encouraging others. Learning to value each other's contributions, listening to peers' comments and building on each other's ideas are central to responding to each other's writing and reading. Talking about books, turn-taking, clarifying ideas and criticising the ideas and not the person are keys to effective book discussions.

BEGINNING CO-OPERATIVE LEARNING

To begin, Lyn wrote a list of co-operative skills the children use in the classroom and playground. This list was framed in positive language, avoiding negative examples like 'no fiddling', 'no wriggling' as this stresses negative behaviour. The negative statements are changed to 'empty hands', 'sit still' because Lyn wants positive examples for the children to follow.

The class brainstormed:

We co-operate when we

- listen
- use quiet voices
- look at eachother
- help
- take turns
- make spaces
- have one person speak

Lyn realised that even though the co-operative skills were identified, many children were uncertain of what it meant, for example, to use quiet voices. Lyn thought about what worked successfully when she introduced some new content in reading, such as recognition of the word 'said'. She wrote the word on the blackboard to make it explicit then gave children lots of practice reading the word in context. Feedback and encouragement were provided after practice. Lyn recalled,

> *As teachers we set aside lots of time for academic learning but less for teaching children how to work co-operatively. We give positive feedback on the academic skills and achievements of children. 'You read that well', 'Yes those words are correct.' Most of us notice co-operative skills when they break down and there is conflict or a behaviour problem. We say 'Don't do that', 'You are not listening.' A better way is to make the co-operative skills explicit and give positive feedback when they occur, just as in academic learning.*

Lyn works with the class to make co-operative skills explicit.

Lyn found that co-operative skills do not happen overnight, nor are they something children are born with. Co-operative skills are learnt from others and we learn and relearn them at different times and in different situations.

A list of co-operative skills can grow over the year.

CO-OPERATIVE SKILLS

FORMING GROUPS
making space for people
making pairs or circles
staying with the group
keeping hands and feet to yourself
forming groups without bothering others

COMMUNICATION
eye contact
taking turns
active listening
using quiet voices
using people's names
eliminating put-downs

WORKING WITH GROUP ROLES
observer
recorder
summariser
encourager
clarifier
organiser
timekeeper

PROBLEM SOLVING AS A GROUP
defining the problem
brainstorming
clarifying ideas
confirming ideas
elaborating ideas
seeing consequences
criticising ideas
organising information
finding solutions

MANAGING DIFFERENCES
stating position or problem
seeing the problem from another view
negotiating
mediating
reaching consensus

MAKING CO-OPERATIVE SKILLS EXPLICIT

Once Lyn decided that teaching co-operative skills was as important as teaching academic skills, she found the process of making the co-operative skill explicit, then providing practice and feedback to be a cornerstone of her teaching. Lyn modified the work of David and Roger Johnson (1989) in developing techniques.

Lyn began in a small way to introduce the way to work together in co-operative learning. She valued partner reading as a way young children can practise reading to one another, with the listener responding with a question about the text. But some of the children in the class read on and on without taking turns. Others didn't listen to their partner's response, too keen on getting ready for their own turn.

Lyn decided to make explicit what is involved in turn-taking. She chose one co-operative skill and the smallest group possible — a pair. Two successful turn-takers were asked to read in the middle of a circle with other children in a fishbowl around them. The class watched.

Natasha: Who wants to go first?
Rebecca: You have first read.
Natasha: How much will I read? It's eight pages long.
Rebecca: The whole book.

The class watches as a co-operative skill is demonstrated.

	Ways of making the co-operative skills explicit
explaining the skill	'When we take turns we wait until the other person has finished talking. We can use eye contact.'
role plays	Children proficient in the particular behaviour are chosen to demonstrate the skill. Others watch. Children like role plays where the teacher takes a role with the children. This works well because the teacher has proficiency in the skill and knows what to stress in the role play.
fishbowl	This is a circle formed around children who are showing how they solve problems or engage in some co-operative skill.
asking the experts	Chairperson of the school council, local MP, principal, or any other member of the community who works in a team, may describe the co-operative skills they use to get their work done.
Y Charts	A chart describing what it feels like / looks like / sounds like. The Y chart contains ideas built up over several days by the children and the teacher.

Natasha: (*reads*)
Rebecca: My question is . . . Where did she find her Mum?
Natasha: In the supermarket. She was there all the time. Your turn to read.

After the role play, Lyn divided a sheet of paper into three and said,

> *Let's build a Y chart about turn-taking. What does it look like to take turns? What does it sound like to take turns, and how does it feel when we take turns?*

The children brainstormed the ideas to add to the chart to make turn-taking explicit.

Lyn developed Y charts as a way of recording co-operative behaviours and making them explicit. The Y charts are displayed in the classroom to remind children to use co-operative skills. Some very complex co-operative skills like negotiating or clarifying are referred to constantly by the class.

PRACTICE

Once the co-operative skill is made explicit, children then practise it. Sometimes Lyn sets a time limit: 'You have five minutes to read. Your partner listens then asks questions.' Lyn walks around commenting on the positive examples of turn-taking she observes.

Lyn acknowledges the students demonstrating the skill.

> *I saw Sam take turns.*
> *Jerri waited till it was his turn.*
> *Natasha watched the time so both people had a turn.*

FEEDBACK

Lyn claims that

> *Time for feedback can be hard to find yet feedback provides clear and tangible evidence about what the teacher values. If a competitive academic curriculum is valued highly, the feedback will stress who succeeded and at what level. If co-operation and supporting others is valued, time will be set aside for describing how we worked. Actions speak louder than words. If we value co-operation, the time set aside for evaluating and providing feedback on how we work is critical.*

Feedback on co-operative skills is important for three reasons.
1. It improves the ways we work together.

2. It encourages individual and group responsibility for using co-operative skills.

3. It maintains the focus on using co-operative skills.

For Lyn,

> *Feedback on the positive examples of co-operative skills is necessary. I comment on the behaviours I want to retain and ignore the rest. It is best if only one or two co-operative skills are a focus. Working on any more leads to skills being forgotten. I am specific about the skills being monitored, for example,*
>   *I saw Simon using eye contact.*
> *Natasha took turns.*
> *Lee asked a question to see if it was his turn.*
> *Rosa said let's take turns.*
> *Brett listened attentively.*

QUICK FEEDBACK IDEAS
Lyn uses several different forms of feedback.

Whip
The whole class or group sits in a circle and each person offers feedback on their individual contribution. Variations include individuals commenting on their peers' efforts, for example, the person on their left. It is important that each group member receives feedback.

Numbered heads
Each person in a group receives a number. The teacher or observer poses a question and all the number 4s give a response.

Checklists
Feedback checklists with space for the skill(s) to be added are given out and students respond either in a group or individually.

Co-operative group goals   Used   Not used

1. Turn-taking
2. No put-downs
3. Criticising ideas not people

As a group member next time *I will listen and ask other people their questions*

FEEDBACK WITH AN OBSERVER
At times an observer can monitor a group and provide feedback. The moment a group is aware that their interactions are being monitored they call on co-operative skills. For children who are less co-operative, taking the role of observer enables them to see how more skilled children negotiate and solve problems. Observers can use feedback checklists. Observers appear to learn more than those involved in the group activity, perhaps because their concentration level is particularly high.

CO-OPERATIVE STRUCTURES
Near the end of a year of co-operative learning, Lyn discovered another powerful idea. Some literacy activities have a structure that more or less ensures that the group has to co-operate to complete the activity. In choral reading, for example, the class was divided into three groups to read:

1   Once upon a time
2   There were three little pigs
3   And all they could say was
All Wee . . . wee.

All have to co-operate for the choral reading to work. The children take turns, listen, encourage each other and remind each other when to join in and what to say. The group sinks or swims together. Creating a play has a similar structure. The children take on a role: props, lighting, sound, director, actors; all work together to create the product, the play performance for others to enjoy.

Lyn found that co-operative structures can help every child participate and take control of the way they learn as individuals or as members of a group. It is positive interdependence that creates the feeling that the group is one unit working together.

Co-operative groups	Traditional groups
• positive interdependence	• no positive interdependence
• common goals	• no common goals
• heterogeneous groups	• homogeneous groups
• shared leadership	• one leader
• frequently changing membership	• static membership
• co-operative skills are taught	• no co-operative skills taught
• group and individual responsibility	• no group or individual responsibility

CO-OPERATIVE STRUCTURES CREATE POSITIVE INTERDEPENDENCE

Positive interdependence occurs when the members of a group of readers or writers understand that they cannot succeed unless the whole group succeeds. If a group sits at the same table, writing about an excursion, talking about what they will write and helping each other with spelling and choice of words, this is a weak form of positive interdependence. The group may be collaborating, with each member contributing to the success of the other members, but the individuals could succeed on their own.

If, on the other hand, a group is creating a newsletter about a class excursion, the work can be divided so that each person contributes, with subtasks like creating a cartoon, writing about a humorous event, making up a puzzle and writing a brief report. The roles of proofreader, layout person, organiser and illustrator can be assigned so the group achieves a polished product and strong, positive interdependence.

Positive interdependence can occur in a number of ways. **Goal interdependence** occurs when a small group of children want to write and perform a play; the group has the same outcome or product in mind. If the group members have differing goals it will be difficult to work co-operatively. Goals can be very broad, with scope left for creativity.

Reward or **recognition interdependence** can focus the group on the literacy product: a class book, a play, a newsletter, a book discussion leading to a group mural. Rewards for the whole group can include stickers, tokens, points or grades. If points are given, individual points may be tallied and divided to create a group score. Recognition interdependence may be having work displayed, shared with others and receiving feedback from peers and the teacher. In reward interdependence, the group receives the same grade or points. Lyn prefers recognition interdependence where the group as a whole is given feedback.

While group recognition and reward is a way of developing positive interdependence, individual accountability also takes place. Lyn sometimes uses numbered heads as a way of encouraging individual

Positive interdependence can arise from shared roles.

accountability. Children in a group may number off 1,2,3,4. Lyn may say,

> *Tell me how your group is working number 4. Tell me what your partner is working on number 2.*

Other forms of interdependence include **resource**, **role** and **work** interdependence which may all overlap. **Work interdependence** occurs when the work subtasks contribute to the whole. **Resource interdependence** could involve having one piece of paper for a class newsletter, one class book compiled from a page from everyone or one computer for the group. **Role interdependence** involves structuring the group so that roles of timekeeper, organiser, convener, etc. are allocated for getting the job done.

Positive interdependence creates eagerness to work together because students feel their effort is indispensable to the group. The following ways of structuring for positive interdependence can be used in literacy learning.

STRUCTURING FOR POSITIVE INTERDEPENDENCE IN LITERACY ACTIVITIES

Co-operative structures allow students to practise co-operative skills as they engage in language and literacy activities. The structures make use of the concept of positive interdependence, and children work in randomly chosen heterogeneous groups.

Lyn chooses heterogeneous mixed-ability groups because children working with others from a range of abilities need to call more on co-operative skills. She randomly groups the class using a deck of cards

> *so that children don't feel socially engineered. Even counting out one, two, one, two can be a set-up. I was a fat kid, always rejected. It is kinder to use a deck of cards.*

Lyn rarely invites the children to work in friendship groups as these do not require the children to use a range of co-operative skills. We can often predict how friends, or people like us, think and act. Self-selected homogeneous groups can leave the less proficient students without academic and social role models as the academically able tend to group together and those with less developed skills are left to form a group. Gifted students benefit from using co-operative skills, and engaging in high level thinking when explaining ideas to those who may not grasp information as quickly.

SOME CO-OPERATIVE STRUCTURES

Think/pair/share

Lyn uses think/pair/share after a group has listened to her read aloud. The children reflect for a minute or two on a question posed by the teacher. These reflections may be written down. The ideas are then shared with a partner. Lyn may ask individuals to paraphrase the ideas given by their partner.

Think/pair/share can be used to gather students' responses or to gather questions readers may pose before reading the next chapter or section. Reactions to writing and feedback to authors about their writing can be gathered in a quick think/pair/share structure. All students contribute rather than one or two more articulate students. (Based on work by Spencer Kagan, 1990.)

Practising the skills.

Think/pair/four/share

Here children reflect for a moment on a particular question or issue, for example from a fable 'The Wolf in Sheep's Clothing' read aloud by Sue Ryan, a Year 6/7 teacher. The moral of this tale is *Pretending to be what you are not leads to trouble*. Sue then asks the students to form pairs. She says, 'You have a minute of think time before sharing ideas. Person A is to describe at least three reasons why pretending to be what you are not does *not* necessarily lead to trouble. Person B in each pair describes three reasons or examples where the moral holds true.'

Each pair joins up with another pair and all take turns reporting by paraphrasing their partner's ideas and responses. The group of four then attempts to reach consensus by combining or synthesising ideas.

A summariser may then provide a summary or consensus of ideas for the class. (Adapted from Spencer Kagan, 1990.)

Three-step interviews

Sue Ryan's class of Year 6 children are exploring how to construct an argument in order to write to the local council about a suggested road closure near the school. Various models of how to construct an argument have been read from the letters to the editor in the local newspaper. These models have been discussed and students now, in pairs, interview each other to discover each other's views about procedures for constructing an argument, to be written in a formal letter to the council. Sue then asks the pair to report to the whole group on the format used in writing an argument.

Alternatively, Sue may have asked for the points for and against the road closure to be gathered with person A taking one side and person B the other. Then the ideas from both could be shared with the class. (Adapted from Spencer Kagan 1990.)

Pyramiding

A modification of three-step interview. After partner work using three-step interviews, groups of four or six join together to pool ideas. The group may work towards consensus on an issue. (Modified from Spencer Kagan.)

Redlight-greenlight thinking

In Jane O'Loughlin's class children are in pairs discussing 'Gruesome fairytales should be banned'. One person has nominated to take the greenlight view and the other the redlight view.

- The greenlight view symbolises growth, creativity, energy and divergent thinking. The greenlight person brainstorms, looks at alternatives and seeks new ideas.
- The redlight view symbolises stop lights, danger, caution, reflection, convergent thinking and examines the consequences of various ideas and actions.

The greenlight person goes first:

> *It is ridiculous to ban fairy tales because the storylines are used again and again in stories. TV plots are much more gruesome. It is an adult view that gruesomeness affects children. Children mostly see gruesomeness as a lot of fun.*

The redlight view continues:

> *We must take care with some young readers not to give ideas that will cause nightmares or emotional disturbance. The violence in gruesome tales can be*

worse than the same TV violence. Gruesomeness in the imagination is worse than gruesomeness in real life.

This structure works best if the greenlight view is gathered first. Once the greenlight brainstorm is exhausted the redlight may step in to examine the consequences of the green suggestions. (From Owen Smith.)

Six hats

Six thinking hats are used in Jane O'Loughlin's class to generate divergent thinking and perspective taking around a text. The co-operative structure offers great possibilities for discussing both informational or narrative texts. An issue such as *Is it possible to find a replacement for logging trees from rainforests?* was discussed after reading the book *Where the Forest Meets the Sea* by Jeannie Baker.

Children in randomly selected groups of six were assigned a coloured hat (either concretely or symbolically).

WHITE HAT: information, facts only, no interpretations or arguments
RED HAT: emotions, how people may feel or how the red hat person personally feels, uses intuitions
PURPLE HAT: caution, judgement, looks at the consequences of any idea or action, is critical and plays devil's advocate
YELLOW HAT: positive optimistic view, looks at the benefits of the idea
GREEN HAT: creative, divergent ideas, brainstorms, offers something that has not been said before
BLUE HAT: encourages others, monitors the process, makes sure each person has a turn, summarises what has been said, decides if people should change hats. (Adapted from Edward de Bono, 1991.)

EEKK

An acronym for sitting eye-to-eye and knee-to-knee. The EEKK structure promotes face-to-face interaction. The role of listener/speaker, interviewer/interviewee or affirmative/negative are assigned and children may be introduced to simple debating skills.

In Jane O'Loughlin's class the children, in groups of six, read a short story. They chose an issue to debate from a novel they were reading, *Was it right for the children to vandalise the kitchen?* The issue has to have two points of view. The group of six split into pairs. One person took an affirmative role and worked out three arguments for *yes*. The other took a negative role and presented three arguments for *no*.

Affirmative and negative roles were switched so both had a turn at exploring an issue from two sides. Then the pair tried to reach a compromise or consensus. The agreement was shared by each pair back in the group of six. (From Dishon and Wilson 1991.)

Whip

Jane, Lyn and Sue use the whip in literacy activities to give quick feedback. A class or small group sits in a circle. Each person contributes an idea or one sentence. Feedback may describe how each person worked in the group, or may be used to set goals.

Sam helped me with a word.
Rebecca chose a book for me.
Nat asked a good question.

Next time we will:
listen to each other,
organise a time keeper,
start on time.

A whip may be a circle where each participant is asked to reflect and predict what a chapter will cover or the plot of a picture book. Sometimes, to speed up responses, a group spokesperson contributes a new idea to a class list of ideas.

Huddle

Like a football huddle, groups join together to answer questions put by the teacher. The teacher may ask the group to predict what the book will be about, to predict what will happen when the page is turned or to suggest how the plot may be resolved. Speed is a factor here and all contribute. Interactive huddles may pose a question to ask other groups or, as a variation, each group may huddle to generate questions for the teacher.

Piggybacking

One of the most difficult things for children to do is to acknowledge the ideas of others. One way to do this is for children to paraphrase the comments of a speaker they agree with and piggyback on the idea. The child may say, 'I agree (or disagree) that . . .,' then their own comments are added.

We all piggyback on each other's ideas and depend on others for feedback on our ideas and for ways of refining and improving our teaching and learning.

Roundtable

In small groups, children share one piece of paper and a marker to record several ideas or answers. The teacher may call on groups to predict what will happen to the character. The group huddles and shares responses. Several responses or one group summary may be recorded.

A version of this is to have one piece of paper and several pens; children write one idea on the piece of paper and pass it to the next person. Children may be in teams recording all the prior knowledge they have about a topic before beginning research or further reading. (Kagan 1990)

Co-operative structures such as piggybacking are made explicit.

Big picture/small picture
This co-operative structure is useful for framing class and group goals. Lyn sees goal interdependence as a requirement for co-operative groups and begins the procedure with the class brainstorming a range of features about a topic — for example, 'What are some of our successful reading behaviours?' or 'How can we tell if a piece of writing is successful?' A list of features is recorded by Lyn. From the brainstormed list or big picture, a small selection or the small picture of achievable goals to work towards is negotiated. These small achievable goals become the focus for Lyn's teaching, to make the ideas explicit, have practice, give feedback and set goals.

Jigsaw
This is a wonderful co-operative structure because each person feels valued by the group as having particular knowledge to contribute. To begin, the class may list poets they like to read:

- Shel Silverstein
- Michael Rosen
- Ogden Nash
- Max Fatchen
- Dennis Lee
- Hilaire Belloc

If there is a class of twenty-five children, five of the poets are selected for study. The class may talk about, then vote on, the favourite five. Children are numbered off 1,2,3,4,5,1,2,3,4,5 . . . and five children are randomly assigned to a research group to study Shel Silverstein — to find what he has written and some biographical details. The next five study Michael Rosen. The next five, Ogden Nash, and so on. Once the research groups have sufficient information, or the time limit has been reached, they re-form into co-operative groups. Each co-operative group has a research expert on Michael Rosen, Ogden Nash, Shel Silverstein, Max Fachen and Dennis Lee. The co-operative groups share information, each member describing information they alone in the group can provide. Often the co-operative groups may construct a poster, a play, a group poem or something similar to share with the class.

Research groups

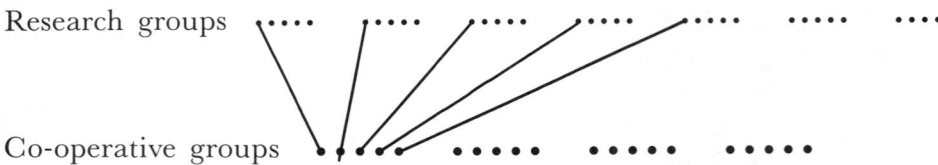

Co-operative groups

When planning the groups it helps to divide the class into groups carefully. If there are twenty children, they can be placed in five expert groups and re-form into four co-operative groups to share ideas. (Based on Aronson, et al. 1977.

CO-OPERATIVE LEARNING BENEFITS LITERACY LEARNING

Lyn is convinced of the value of co-operative literacy learning because it increases the amount of purposeful classroom talk. Students are engaged in deeper levels of thinking and reflection which promotes learning. Communication skills are increased as children listen to and describe their thoughts and ideas about reading and writing.

For Lyn,

> *Language is power. Being explicit about the content of what is learned and the way we work together helps children to access the mainstream culture. We are making the culture explicit. We are not teaching people to be compliant. We are involving all children in learning literacy and they help each other.*

PROMOTING LEARNING

Talking about the way we read and write promotes elaboration, clarification and awareness of metacognitive strategies. Metacognitive language in literacy involves the description of and the ability to reflect on and choose a range of strategies and processes we can engage in as we read and write. When others in the group challenge us to prove our ideas or to clarify our meaning we paraphrase, reorganise ideas and explain our thinking processes using examples to get the ideas across. We may expand on how we have formed ideas about the text, substantiate our ideas by rereading particular paragraphs or invite others to reread again taking a different interpretation or different point of view.

Researchers comparing cognitive gains from co-operative, individualistic and competitive classroom structures claim that students retain more, generate more new ideas and solve problems faster in co-operative groups. Numerous studies investigating theories of how children learn, particularly Piaget's cognitive development theory and Kohlberg's moral development theory, indicate that higher level reasoning is promoted when students work co-operatively (Johnson and Johnson 1990).

COMMUNICATION SKILLS

When children work together in book discussions or editing conferences, both reading and writing are enriched by the children's spoken language. When we ask another writer to clarify information, the writer has to struggle a little to understand our point of view and find the words to explain what has not been said. As writers, we may have to paraphrase a sentence and find a more concise way of presenting an idea. We may criticise the way a novel concludes and point out what is unresolved and make suggestions for other conclusions.

Communication is interactive and dynamic. A reader may clarify and gather their own ideas about a book like *The Great Gilly Hopkins,* while expressing their ideas to a co-operative group. Listeners form questions as they listen:

> *Why do you think Gillie Hopkins did that?*
> *What if her foster mother didn't want her?*
> *How could Pete be trapped in the cellar for such a long time?*

As the speaker explains, paraphrases and searches for new examples, they are also considering the listeners' perspectives to better contribute to their understanding.

INCREASED PARTICIPATION

In classrooms we have a range of academic, cultural and linguistic differences and engaging all children is important for academic and social growth.

In a co-operative classroom, the teacher sets aside time for learning alone and learning with others. When a question is asked, a simple co-operative structure like think/pair/share is used so that everyone contributes. The teacher says,

> *Think about what happened in the last chapter. You have a minute to recall as much information as possible . . . With a partner take turns to share what you remember from the last chapter. Each add new information . . . Now, form a group of four and paraphrase what your partner remembered . . . Number off 1 to 4 . . . Could the number 2s in the group summarise what the group recalled . . .*
>
> *I would like to give some feedback on what I saw. Tony waited for Lou Ming to finish her statement. Sardi listened carefully and used her own words to explain Frank's ideas. Everyone remembered a lot from the last chapter.*

In a co-operative classroom there is greater equity of participation. The teacher structures for co-operative learning and observes pairs and groups in action. The co-operative group is structured differently from traditional groups and has different outcomes.

Traditional	Co-operative
• one person speaks	• everyone speaks
• no think time	• time to think
• unequal participation	• equal participation
• same children do the talking	• all have a turn
• no accountability	• everyone listens to paraphrase partner's ideas.

(Based on Kagan 1990)

Lyn discovered that just putting children into groups does not, in itself, promote learning, increase communications skills or encourage equal participation. Traditional grouping often led to 'free riders' saying 'Leave it to Jim'. The workhorse often said, 'Give it to me, I'll do it quickly.' Sometimes the most able, on a particular task, may expend less effort to avoid the 'sucker effect' of doing all the work (Kerr 1982). High ability group members may take over the important leadership roles that benefit them, at the expense of other group members, leading to the 'rich get richer' effect. The more articulate may do all the talking and, since the amount of talking correlates highly with the amount learnt, the more able learn more while the less able flounder as a captive audience (Johnson and Johnson 1990).

Groups perform best when the perceived status of high and low achievers does not direct the interaction of the group, and this is where co-operative learning and co-operative structures have a huge role to play. Learning *how to work together* can be as important as *what we learn*.

In a research project exploring book clubs, where heterogeneous groups of students talked with their classmates about literature, Taffy E. Raphael (1992) and others found that readers in mainstream and special education classrooms benefited from instruction about *what to share* in the book discussion groups and also *how to share* ideas, like taking turns, listening to each other, clarifying ideas and relating comments to ideas raised by another student in discussion. One of the book club students, Mei, described in a letter to an author of a book she had read, '. . . we learn how to talk about this story and think about the story.' Raphael notes that reading had become more than a time to sit silently, say all the words right, and correctly answer the questions. Reading and writing are enriched by co-operative learning.

Children learn how to work together and share ideas as they participate in book discussion groups.

4
SETTING AND MEETING GOALS: READING

♦

Many teachers find that while reading may be a rewarding, solitary experience in itself, learning to read is enriched when children share their interpretations of texts and elaborate on each other's responses.

In Lyn Thompson's class, the five- and six-year-old children sit on the floor, while Lyn arranges a big book of raps and rhymes for the class to read. The big book, compiled by the class, has spring-back rings to allow the children to add or take out pages. The book is a collection of playground chants and group rhymes for everyone to read and join in. The chants were collected out in the school yard, or found in song and poetry books. Lyn writes them up in large print on coloured cardboard. They may have word play, a strong rhythm, easy rhyme, humour, and are often about food. The children like tricky words — no 'baby stuff' — and according to Lyn it is 'cool' to chant 50s and 60s songs like 'Rockin' Robin' and 'Rock around the clock'. On this day Lyn flipped open the book to Mary's choice and said,

> *We are going to try group reading. The people on this side of the group please read the lines with numbers, like one, two, three, four and so on. The other half of the group read the line after the numbers. We'll join in on the last line 'Hungry again'. Ready everyone!*

One, two
Chocolate goo
Three, four

        Want some more
        Five, six
        Pudding mix
        Seven, eight
        Bring your plate
        Nine, Ten
All Hungry again.

Great everyone. Let's repeat it starting softly and getting louder.

GOALS AND STRATEGIES FOR TEACHING READING

Group choral reading helps meet one of Lyn's goals for reading. Lyn, Sue Ryan, Deirdre Travers, Lorraine Leinert and Jane O'Loughlin, are teachers whose ideas, described here, help us to recognise the value of a co-operative classroom community for achieving goals in reading through experiences that are structured so that children learn from many other readers.

Children share raps and rhymes from the class collection.

READING AND WRITING COMMUNITIES

The 'successful behaviours' book helps to make the behaviours explicit.

Specific goals and strategies for co-operative reading	
Appreciating a range of purposes for reading	Raps and rhymes Range sheet Teacher reads aloud Readers theatre
Providing reading practice	Partner reading Paired reading Exchange reading
Valuing and extending children's responses to reading	Literature roulette Author jigsaw Piggybacking Book shares Book discussion Shared reading logs
Improving reading strategies	Predictagloss RRRR
Peer and self-evaluation of reading	Role reading Home response books

TEACHING STRATEGIES FOR CO-OPERATIVE READING

RAPS AND RHYMES

The value of reading for fun and enjoyment as a group is obvious. As well, the class becomes a co-operative, cohesive group of readers as they take turns, join in with soft to loud reading or all chant, clap and click fingers with a loud chorus.

RANGE SHEET

In order to build up a list of the huge range of reading done for different purposes, Lyn's class sat in a circle and brainstormed all the different forms of texts that they read at home and school. Lyn called this brainstormed list a **range sheet** and this gave the class the big picture of all the types or forms of reading children may do. A survey sheet was created from the range sheet and children and parents were invited to fill it in to see just what kind of reading was done at home. The original range sheet was displayed in the classroom for Lyn and the children to refer to during the term to make sure that a range of different kinds of texts were read.

```
What kind of texts does your child read at home?
1.  TV guides          0    10. Newspapers         0
2.  Birthday cards     0    11. Songs              0
3.  Picture books      0    12. Own notes          0
4.  Lists              0    13. Words on T-shirts  0
5.  Jokes              0    14. School notices     0
6.  Clothing labels    0    15. Television         0
7.  Video reviews      0    16. Comics             0
8.  Blackboard         0    17. Jar labels         0
9.  Rhymes             0    18. Posters            0
                            19. Magazines          0
```

When the children returned their completed survey sheets, they used them to make a bar graph of the kinds of text the class could read. Lyn had prepared a large sheet with all the types of texts from the survey sheet listed at the top. The children who needed help to read their survey sheet were asked to find someone to help them. The children each collected a handful of coloured plastic counters and sat on the floor in pairs, to tally the results.

The exercise was a triumph of class co-operation. As Lyn read each item the children with that item ticked placed a counter in a line under that item on the large sheet. Most of the pairs sat with a finger slowly moving down each item so they did not lose their place. The class worked briskly; after sixteen minutes the graph was completed, with 150 counters placed on the graph.

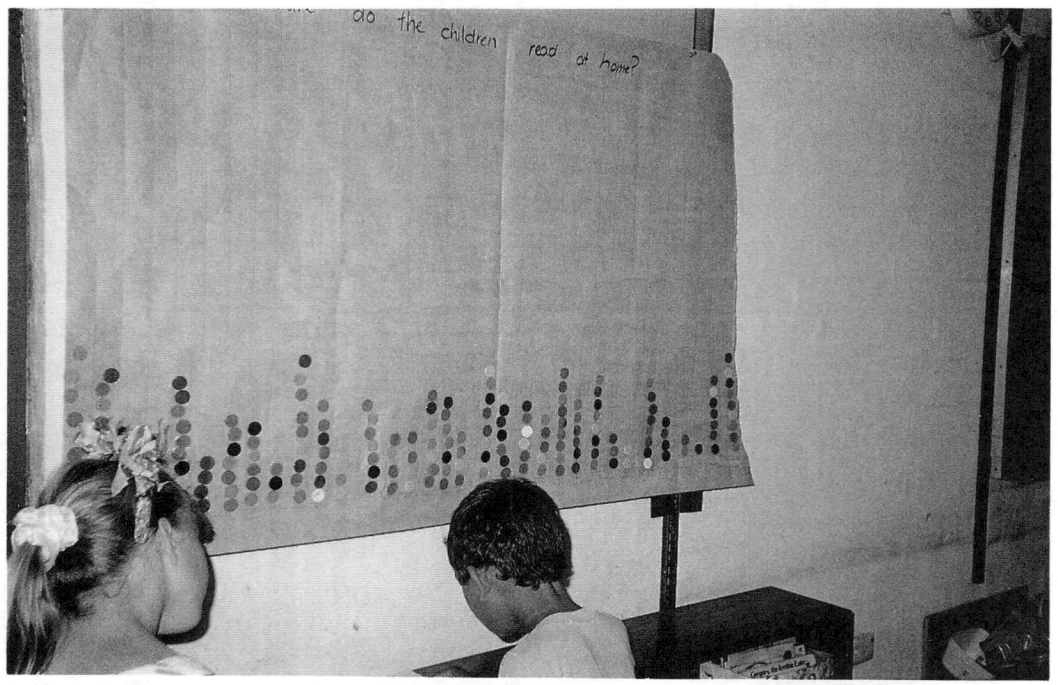

A bar graph showing types of texts read at home was the result of a co-operative class activity.

Clear tape was placed over the counters and the class then had a bar graph displaying the variety of texts read.

Lyn makes a variety of text types available whenever there is free choice reading — at least once a day. There are cards, catalogues, magazines, comics, non-fiction, poetry, TV guides, the raps and rhymes big book, as well as picture books.

TEACHER READS ALOUD

Many teachers read aloud to the class several times a day, time permitting. Sue Ryan, a Year 7 teacher, claims that literature is not as important as TV in the children's life and culture outside school. She works hard to find books to read aloud that will work. Novels dealing with peer pressure, family conflict and humour catch the children's imagination and interest.

Sue asks questions to build a bridge from the book to the children's experiences by asking questions like, *Has this happened to you? Have you let yourself be bullied?* She asks the group to think/pair/share a response, to encourage all children to think and answer. Children responded:

There was a time when all the kids got on to me. The shock stopped me. I thought about it afterwards.

Why did she let him grab her? I would have thumped him.

When I was in Year Two a Year Seven leather jacket chased me. He bullied me and I let him.

By sharing knowledge and feelings about life experiences prompted by the story read aloud, children are making connections with each other and building a bank of shared experiences.

READERS THEATRE

Readers theatre is a way of making texts come alive through performance. Picture books, poems, novels and play scripts may be developed into a readers theatre performance to show other groups and other classes. Less proficient readers are not left on the sidelines and the confidence of all readers increases because of repeated reading.

Readers theatre provides for reading practice through repeated rereading of a text. Children also develop the ability to discuss how language works and are encouraged to explore the structure of a text.

The co-operative goals in readers theatre include turn-taking, brainstorming, reaching consensus about performance styles and criticising ideas and not the person. There are also group roles to play such as timekeeper, organiser, director, props, producer and script checker.

Most teachers begin readers theatre by demonstrating with repetitive picture books like *Hattie and the Fox* by Mem Fox or *Who Sank the Boat?* by Pamela Allen. The teacher reads the text through first of all, then invites the children to join in on the dialogue or alternate sentences to create a performance or readers theatre.

Groups then select a picture book from many supplied. They read the books through and decide which book best suits performance. They then practise the performance until it goes well, and they are ready to show others what they have developed.

A set of criteria to look for or features used in an effective readers theatre performance may be brainstormed, and groups can provide feedback on each other's performance.

PROVIDING READING PRACTICE

PARTNER READING

To get started, Lyn asks two proficient readers to sit in the centre of a fishbowl with the other children in a circle around them. The children in the circle are observers, watching for the behaviour partners use when reading together. Lyn assigns two roles, a reader and a questioner. Each person will read and the other asks questions about the text.

Making reading strategies explicit

Lyn explains that after watching the partners the group will make a Y chart about what partner reading looks, sounds, and feels like. 'Everyone will have an idea to record on the Y chart,' Lyn reminds them.

READING AND WRITING COMMUNITIES

A Y chart for partner reading leads to a listing of successful strategies.

After watching the partners take turns to read and ask questions, Lyn and the children build up a Y chart. From the huge list of behaviours on the Y chart Lyn asks the children to select the most important successful behaviours for partner reading.
This list of reading strategies is displayed in the classroom and the children refer to it when they need to help their partner.

Practice
Now it's time for everyone to practise. Children each choose a book from their book box. Lyn also includes books from her personal library in the partner reading book boxes. She has another set of books for children to take home and read.

SETTING AND MEETING GOALS: READING

Reading strategies

- go back and reread it
- ask for help (reread)
- look at the picture
- point to the exact part of the picture
- spell / sound the word
- tell them the first letter
- give a prediction

READING MUST MAKE SENSE

Cream: books with few words, predictable words and phrases for emergent readers.
Yellow: books with one/three sentences per page, repetition, and often a predictable structure for beginning/fluent readers.
Green: books with more complex vocabulary and syntax for more rapid readers.

In partner reading today the children have been assigned a partner for some of these reasons:
- confident reader helps a less confident reader
- friendship pairs work with some children
- similar reading ability pairs provide good practice
- confident strong reader challenges another confident strong reader

- pairs of mixed gender and cultural backgrounds provide practice of co-operative skills

The children in pairs quickly sit 'side by side, knee-to-knee' so that concentration and listening to each other is easy. The reader reads, then the questioner asks a question at the end of the reading. Lyn says questioning always needs a lot of practice but most of her class are familiar with 'who', 'what', 'when', 'where' and 'how' as a memory trigger for asking questions.

Feedback

'Let's have a quick whip around for feedback,' Lyn suggests. Time is short. The children look at the Y chart and the list of successful behaviours for reading. Each person then says something different about what their partner did that helped them.

Tom helped me work out a word.
Simon listened to me all the time.

Sometimes Lyn asks for feedback on specific co-operative behaviours,

I saw Mary put her hand out to a partner.
Simon sat down quickly with Trish.

and sometimes for feedback on the reading strategies practised in the lesson. Another time she might ask children to give feedback by saying the title of their partner's book and one sentence about it. This encourages children to pay attention to what their partner is reading and provides practice at summarising information. For example, Bill said,

Simon's book is 'Where's Kevin' and it's about a kangaroo who goes to different places.

Partner reading can look easy but Lyn says that children need lots of practice forming partnerships. Sometimes Lyn structures partner work so that children select and work with up to four different partners in one session. In building a community of readers, the successful co-operative skills for working together *and* the successful reading strategies are made explicit, that is — **how** we work together and **what** we learn.

PAIRED READING

This is sometimes called cross-age tutoring where children of mixed ages read together. Both bring a book for the younger reader to read. Teachers and librarians find it useful to work on book selection — using the blurb, reading the first few pages, using the five finger test where a finger is put down for each unknown word. In a passage of twenty words in a picture book one finger down amounts to an accuracy rate of approximately 95%. Five fingers down in one hundred words is also 95% accuracy.

'The greatest benefits occur for the "teacher" so less proficient older readers reap most from this procedure,' says Sue Ryan, whose older readers, eleven- and twelve-year-olds, work with Lyn Thompson's five- and six-year-old children. Sue says,

> *It is something they love and will do for twenty to twenty-five minutes unsupervised. They check out up to six books for the younger reader. I hear them saying, 'Can you reread that?' 'Skip the word and come back to it later.' 'Well, look at the first sound, what do you think it says?' The children know all the strategies like encouraging, looking at the pictures, rereading, finger pointing. They know how to ask questions. We have a feedback circle with the tutors to keep the focus on using co-operative skills and successful reading strategies to use.*

Procedures for paired reading

Cross-age reading occurred between all classes at Taperoo. The teachers agreed to use a similar process to coach all children. First children read a book together. Usually the more proficient reader reads out aloud while the other child joins in when they feel confident. There are arranged cues between the readers. When one reader knocks on the table this is a signal that they want to read alone.

EXCHANGE READING

This strategy can be used as a format for taking turns in paired reading or in partner reading.

Prepare	1. Both readers A and B select a text within their reading level and interests.
	2. Negotiate how much each will read.
Predict	3. A asks B to predict what the text will be about. Use the title and pictures as a guide.
	4. B reads agreed amount.
Clarify	5. A asks for clarification of word meanings or ideas in the text.
Question	6. A asks a 'W' question or a generic question like 'What did the book remind you of?' or a question of their choice.
Summarise	7. B summarises the main ideas in the text. The summary should contain all the important ideas.
	8. Reverse roles and B asks A to predict what the next part of the story will be about.

Repeated co-operative reading provides the more reluctant readers with support to practise the strategies they need to gain fluency, while also building confidence.

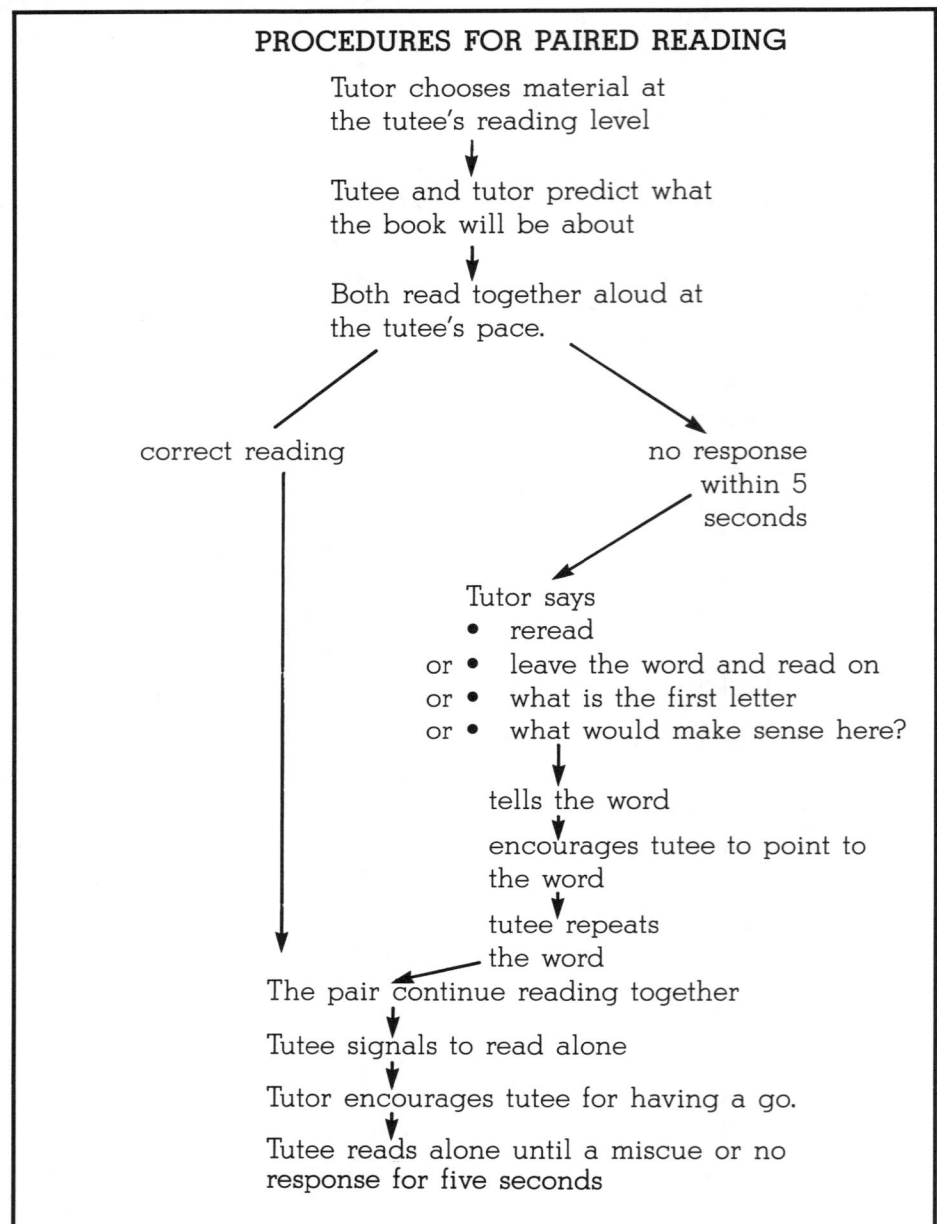

VALUING AND EXTENDING RESPONSES

LITERATURE ROULETTE

In literature roulette, groups of five or six children discuss a book they are reading. The group may meet weekly to discuss a novel, chapter by chapter. The roulette wheel has open-ended questions based on Bloom's taxonomy of educational objectives (1956). The questions have been designed to suit any book. Questions may include some of the following:

- knowledge questions: recalling information
  What problems did the main character face?
  Describe the main events.
  Describe a time line of events in order.
  Describe a character.
- comprehension questions: understanding meaning
  Retell the story in your own words.
  Describe your favourite section.
  Describe why the main character(s) behaved as they did.
  Give an example of a character's feeling.
- application questions: using learning in a new situation
  Explain how you could use an idea from the book.
  If you were one of the characters would you do the same?
  What would you do if you were in the book?
  How would you solve this problem in your own life?
- analysis questions: ability to see parts and relationships
  What caused the main character to act in this way?
  What things could not happen in real life?
  Is this book/chapter like another?
  What do you predict will happen next? Why?
- synthesis questions: parts of information are used to create an original whole
  What is the theme or message so far?
  What would it be like to be in this story?
  Create a new book or chapter ending.
  Add a new idea that was not in the story.
- evaluation questions: judgement based on criteria
  Did you like the story? Why/why not?
  Would you recommend this to a friend? Why/why not?
  Select the best event. Why is this the best?
  Are the characters and events believable?

If the roulette wheel has twelve sections then use a spinner with twelve sections, or a twelve-sided die. The children take turns to answer a question.

Preparation for literature roulette occurs in the week before the meeting. Children must be prepared to answer *any* question on the wheel. Children listen to the group members answer a question. The person on the left of the speaker answering the question poses a further question, asking for clarification or elaboration to extend everyone's understanding of the book.

Teachers demonstrate how to play Literature Roulette in a fishbowl with a group of five or six readers. All readers have agreed upon the number of pages or chapters to read before the meeting.

After each person has spun the spinner or rolled the die and answered a question, each person gives feedback to a group member on what they contributed. Then goals are set for how much to read before the next meeting.

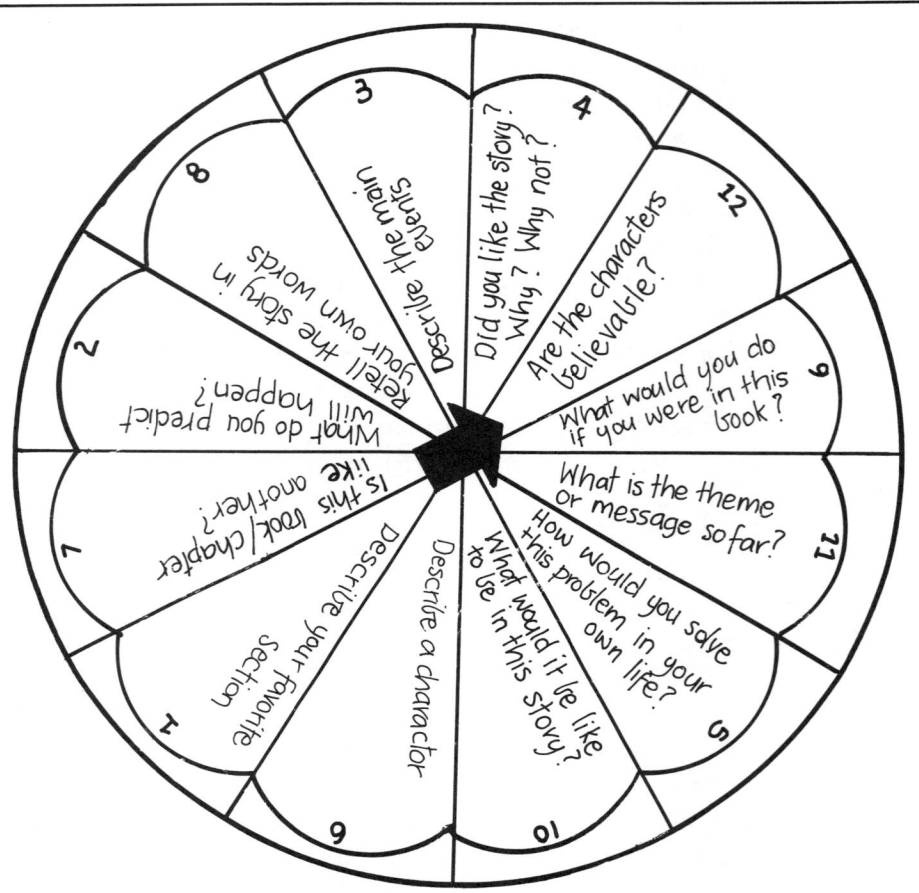

AUTHOR JIGSAW

Author jigsaw is one way of introducing a new author to children as well as extending on the responses children can make to books. Close exploration of texts to find out 'how the author gets us in' provides children with language to use to describe the author's craft. Describing the literary techniques like figurative language, adjectives and imagery, and analysing the character and plots used by different authors enriches children's responses.

Sue Ryan found that many reluctant readers plateau with a favourite author or with a series. To extend their reading selection, Sue and the class made a list of favourite authors. Sue then added a few authors of her choice to extend the range.

SETTING AND MEETING GOALS: READING

Close exploration of texts provides children with language to describe the author's craft and enriches their responses.

Author posters increase the children's range of possible authors.

The list of authors was narrowed down to six so that children could gather and share
- autobiographical details
- lists of books published
- a small selection of the text that demonstrates how the author writes
- how the author gets us in — author's craft.

Children were randomly assigned to six research groups to gather information on one of these authors — Susan Cooper, Anne Martin, Roald Dahl, Betsy Byars, Robin Klein and Anthony Browne. The group members divided responsibility for finding books read, biographical details in library reference books, examples of how the writer writes, and author craft. This research took a one-hour reading session. Next session the different sets of information were shared with another group and *each* group member made an author poster.

The members of the research groups then formed co-operative groups — each with a Betsy Byars expert, an Anne Martin expert, a Susan Cooper expert, and so on. The experts showed their poster and described the information they had compiled collaboratively.

The author posters were displayed in the classroom, and the range of possible authors for children to read is increased.

PIGGYBACKING

When children read and share ideas about books they learn to take account of each other's ideas and base their own responses on what their peers have contributed. One strategy to encourage building on each other's ideas is piggybacking.

We all build on each other's ideas. The important point is to acknowledge another's ideas and say whether we agree or not.

> *I agree that [repeat idea]*
> *Yes I think that [paraphrase idea]*
> *Yes your idea [repeat idea] could work and [extend idea].*
>
> *I think the idea [repeat idea] could work but I disagree that . . .*
> *No I think the idea [repeat idea] is wrong because . . .*
> *The idea to [repeat idea] is fine but I differ on . . .*

It is best to introduce this technique with a simple example. Jane O'Loughlin wrote the above suggestions for piggybacking on the blackboard and then asked two children to discuss the games that can be played in fitness.

> **Chris**: Let's play a different game from cricket in fitness.
> **Howard**: Yes, a different game like Danish rounders would be great.

SETTING AND MEETING GOALS: READING

>**Chris**: Danish rounders would be good. Do you think we've got enough people?

Jane gave feedback to Chris and Howard. So that the class could practise the technique, Jane then read the picture book *Gorilla* by Anthony Browne. Then children were paired as Jane numbered off, 1,2,1,2,1,2 ... Each pair role played the two characters in *Gorilla*, one, Hannah, a young girl who wants to see more of her father, and the other, the father, who works day and night and has little time for her.

The class discussed the story from two points of view, piggybacking on each other's ideas.

'*Spotlight*,' said Jane which is a way of asking a pair or group to demonstrate what they are doing. In the spotlight two children revealed their clever language play.

>**Hannah**: Dad, I know there is a recession but I do want to go and see the gorilla at the zoo.
>
>**Father**: I know you want to see the gorilla at the zoo. Once I get to be manager I will have some more time.
>
>**Hannah**: Oh Dad, I know you want to get to be manager but it is my childhood fantasy to go to the zoo.
>
>**Father**: I realise this is a childhood fantasy. Oh dear, maybe I can find some time on your birthday. My boss gives me time off for someone's birthday or when they get married.

The class laughs. In a whip around the circle, as feedback for the group, Jane asked each of the twenty-eight children to describe something they learnt from the session. Comments included:

Books have different points of view
How to piggyback
Not to put people down
To accept another person's opinion
When I'm with a partner not to make faces

How to paraphrase
If you don't go crazy you get your work done quicker
How to listen
How to get into being the character
Working with people who aren't your friends
Clarifying what people say

Piggybacking is used over and over in book discussions and encourages children to listen, take each other seriously, and to link or build on each other's ideas.

BOOK SHARES

In Jane O'Laughlin's classroom, book shares are important for extending the children's choice of books to read. Book shares are conducted in groups with children recording ideas on long pieces of paper about thirty centimetres across and as long as you like. The book shares are placed at corners of the classroom. The title written on the top of each book share varies:

Once a week children are given ten or so minutes to record their opinions on the lists. They are randomly numbered off, grouped, then randomly assigned to a book share list. Four or five children then gather by a book share list, with the books they are reading. Using texta colour markers, they record the title, author and the piece of dialogue, the conflict, character or whatever the list requires.

Time is given during the week to read other children's responses so that information for decisions about what books to read next are shared.

SETTING AND MEETING GOALS: READING

BOOK DISCUSSIONS

Book discussions provide opportunities for readers to express and clarify their own views, to reflect on the reactions of others, and to gain deeper understandings of literature. However, this will only occur where the readers respect each other and feel secure enough to express their own tentative views, to raise opposing viewpoints and to challenge others who hold differing points of view.

Deirdre Travers, a teacher-librarian, introduced a set of books to eleven- and twelve-year-old readers based on a variety of themes to interest the age group. During the term the students met in groups

Book discussions provide opportunities for readers to gain deeper understandings of literature.

READING AND WRITING COMMUNITIES

Preparation for book discussions.

to talk about the titles they had found particularly interesting and to discuss the book in relation to a theme. For the theme 'Growing Up' they discussed the choices and challenges that the characters faced and the ways they saw the characters change. On the theme 'Country Life/City Life' they could make comparisons and relate their own experiences to those they read about. With 'The Environment' as a theme, they shared their understandings of the way the environment shapes the way we live, and the impact of people on the environment.

Each group then reported back to the whole class. The readers gained a greater appreciation of the books read and the variety of responses, and learnt to value each other's recommendations. These guided their selection of books from the thirty to forty titles provided.

Deirdre divided the classes randomly into groups so that students shared their views with a range of other students — not just their friends.

The literature groups were positively interdependent and individual accountability was encouraged. Students had to take turns and listen carefully to each other's contributions: an answer to a question Deirdre set. For example, when reading books based on the theme 'Growing Up', each group member had to decide: *Which character in the books you have read has changed the most?* After several characters were described, the group selected the most changed character to describe to the rest of the class. In the group reading on the theme of 'The Environment', each group member selected an answer to *What is the most effective description in the books read?* The group as a whole then decided on which description to read to the class.

SHARED READING LOGS

Spending ten minutes after silent reading to write reflections and responses to what they have just read is becoming recognised as a valuable strategy for young readers to gain more from their reading (Hansen 1987, Atwell 1987).

Lorraine Leinert, who teaches ten-year-old children, was able to extend the idea of reading logs to build cohesion and co-operation in her class.

First she modelled the behaviour she wanted by reading silently herself, keeping a log and occasionally reading from it to the class. Class members were invited to read aloud their written responses to the whole class. Lorraine commented on the honesty and exploration in the responses and wrote positive responses to each child's written reactions.

When the class members knew the sorts of written comments that were appropriate, she invited them to swap their reading logs with others and write reactions to each other's entries. It was clear from the children's comments that they had learnt the sorts of supportive comments that were desirable, and that they were taking positive responses as recommendations to read the books.

At the end of fifteen weeks of writing regularly in their logs and sharing them, Lorraine reported that the class showed a greater appreciation of each other's views than other classes she had had, more reliance on each other for recommendations of books, more interest in each other's opinions, not only in relation to books, and a higher priority given to reading among the class members (Hancock 1989).

> Today I'm still reading Alison Ashley!! It's great. I've really enjoyed it. So I'm going to keep reading it. Today Erica & Alison had a fight they were calling each other Snobs, showoffs ect. It was quite funny. that part reminded me of how my brother and me fight over something little. There was another part where Barry Hollis put a light thing in the dark room so it kept flashing a light while they were developing the photos. It reminded me of my brother who got some photo's back yesterday who lives in balaklava. I feel Great 😊
>
> Keep reading! I've seen the play and it was great. Perhaps it will come back again. I really enjoy reading your Reading Log, Linda. Ms Dienert

SETTING AND MEETING GOALS: READING

IMPROVING READING STRATEGIES

PREDICTAGLOSS

To begin the predictagloss lesson, Lyn Thompson selects the book *The Bad Tempered Ladybird* by Eric Carle. She plans to read the book aloud, but first shows the cover of the book to the children, then reads the title and back cover blurb. Lyn explains that everyone can try to predict the story content and key words in the book. Lyn reminds the class that they can predict from the cover, title and blurb of the book. She asks the whole group to think for a moment, alone, about what the book will be about, then go with a pair and take turns to share ideas.

Lyn reminds the children of the co-operative skills to use to work together.
- all ideas will be accepted
- no put-downs

Next a foursome is made and ideas are further shared.

The class resumes to make a circle and Lyn records the children's predictions on a chart.

DICTAGLOSS for The bad tempered ladybird

We predict the story will be about

- a ladybird who doesn't share
- a ladybird who found a house and didn't share
- a ladybird who couldn't fight
- the ladybird is told how to share

What words do you predict will be in the book?

lady	food	hate
lazy	fight	naughty
good	animals	tempered
hit	ladybird	

Lyn read the book and asked the children an open-ended response question such as 'What did you like about the book?' Then a knowledge question 'Did the book remind you of another book, *The Very Hungry Caterpillar*, by Eric Carle?'

Then Lyn reviewed the predictagloss predictions. 'Let's check to see if our story predictions were right?' Some predictions were confirmed with a tick and others were crossed off. Then the class reviewed their key word predictions, ticking those the children agreed were in the book.

Predictagloss provides support for all children, both confident readers and those who require more support, because the children think individually of their predictions, share in pairs, then form a four. When the teacher calls for predictions, individuals can contribute ideas from friends. When predictions are checked off individuals do not feel that they were right or wrong as the ideas are a collaborative effort.

Predictagloss can be used in many different ways. The teacher can ask for predictions for fiction or non-fiction texts. In both cases the class predicts both the content and key words.

In another form of predictagloss, the teacher reads aloud a short non-fiction text and children note down key words as they listen. Then the text, with key words deleted as in cloze procedure, is given to pairs of children so they co-operatively complete the gaps. Pairs can then exchange papers with another pair to check their work. To build in individual accountability and encourage self-assessment the teacher may provide each pair with half the key words on a master sheet. Another pair has the other half of the key words. Pairs then work together to complete the task.

RRRR (REFLECT, READ, RECORD AND RESPOND)

Sue Ryan introduced RRRR as a group reading process to build children's repertoire of reading strategies, to boost their attitudes to reading, and as a way of supporting less proficient readers.

Ability grouping in reading had been second nature for most of the eleven- and twelve-year-olds. Everyone knew who was a good reader and who wasn't. In RRRR, proficient and less confident readers were randomly placed in groups of six. Sue modelled the strategies many times before she was comfortable with the idea that children could manage on their own. Groups stayed together for a ten-week term or until two books were read. The group decided how much to read each session and chose the group book to read in consultation with Sue.

Reflect

Children were asked to reflect for a minute on what the book or the next chapter will be about, using the title, illustrations and the blurb as a basis for predictions. The predictions were then shared around the group.

SETTING AND MEETING GOALS: READING

Read

Working in pairs the children read together. They took turns to read aloud—a paragraph each, or one read the dialogue while the other the descriptions. Time was set aside in reading time for this. Sue did not assume that time to read at home was possible for all children.

Record

Here the class records the words they did not understand. Sometimes they looked up the meaning of the words in the dictionary or other sources.

Respond

The children respond in a journal. At the conclusion of the book they could illustrate, write or create some form of response either individually or as small groups.

Sue commented that it pays off to persist when children experience a lot of conflict when first working together. There were some children in the class who had chosen not to read for many years.

> *When we began, some kids, given a choice, just wouldn't read a book. So I didn't give them that choice. They had to have a go at reading a book. Some groups started out with a picture book or a magazine. A novel was too daunting for them. When faced with a novel they would say in the first chapter, 'I'm not interested in the book' or 'It's boring' or 'Too hard'. This put me and other children in an uncomfortable position about reading*

> *Some of these kids have chips on their shoulders. They're angry at some deal life's given them, moving around a bit from school to school. Sometimes they act tough yet anything new will frighten them to tears.*

> *I talk a lot about why I'm doing what I'm doing. I refer continually to my goals, why I'm teaching them to work together, why we're learning what we're learning, what use it will be to them. I hope they're setting their goals as well. They haven't had a lot of being talked to like this. Now they ask me, Why are we doing this Mrs Ryan? What's the point of learning this? I like that.*

The RRRR process took a long time to refine. In the beginning it took three sessions for the group to agree on what book to read. In the first term of the school year most groups chose easy-to-read picture books to get through quickly. By fourth term they all chose novels. The groups set goals for what to read, how much to read and what kind of response to make. Responses are often brief feedback sessions but, at the conclusion of the book, more large-scale projects like a poster or model may be jointly constructed. Parents were involved in RRRR as they read and made comments in the response journal. Sue noted this response from a new parent at the school: 'My child is reading at home for the first time.'

PEER AND SELF-EVALUATION

ROLE READING

When we read we predict the content of the story or information from the cover, title, headings and illustration. Often we pose questions about the content of the text while reading or after reading an extract. Summarising the ideas so far allows us to gather the main ideas before reading on. Clarifying concepts or ideas, unfamiliar vocabulary, unclear word meanings and syntax helps the reader comprehend the text.

Each of these strategies, **predicting**, **questioning**, **summarising** and **clarifying**, promotes both comprehension of a text and comprehension monitoring. Annemarie Palincsar and Ann Brown (1986) developed a technique called reciprocal teaching where students are given demonstrations of how predicting, questioning, summarising and clarifying can be used to help them to understand texts.

The strategies of reciprocal teaching can be adapted to role reading where students in groups of four transform the strategies into roles performed by each reader. One reader is the predictor, another the questioner, a third the summariser and a fourth the clarifier.

One role is introduced each day and modelled to the class. To demonstrate prediction the teacher may say, 'How do I predict what this book will be about? What clues do I have? In what form or genre will the book be written? What will the book cover?' After this initial discussion, the prediction questions are written on the blackboard.

On further days the other strategies are demonstrated. Many teachers use the idea of **five w's** to help children generate questions based on *why, who, when, what, where*. Open and closed questions and interpretive, critical and evaluative questions may be modelled and asked after the text has been read. Summarising the main ideas, rather than retelling of endless details, can be difficult for some children, so practice can be done first with picture books to allow children to grasp the concept of summary.

Examples of the language that each person might use can be listed on a chart.

Predictor
What do I think . . .?
What ideas or information will the book cover?
In what form or genre will the book be written?
Who will be in the story?
Where will it happen?
Why will this occur?

Questioner
Why did this event happen?

Have you experienced anything like this?
Does this remind you of anything?
If you had to explain . . . what would you say?
What were the most important ideas?

Summariser
The main ideas were . . .
The gist of the story so far is . . .
The book/page/article was about ...
In summary the information says ...

Clarifier
Were the ideas clear?
Were there words anyone did not understand or couldn't read?
Can anyone explain what ... means?

Role reading can be used in ability groups or mixed ability groups. Sue Ryan had five ability groups of four people. Each group read a different book. One group read *Unbelievable!* by Paul Jennings. They had a tape recording of the book as they were not independent readers. Another group of keen series readers read a Babysitter Club book by Ann Martin. A group of proficient readers read *So Much To Tell You* by John Marsden. *Going Solo* by Roald Dahl was read by a group of Dahl fans and Gillian Rubinstein's book, *Flashback*, was read by another group of proficient readers.

The group decided how much they would read before discussing the book. In some groups the students decided to read aloud, taking turns with a partner. Others chose to read silently. Some groups read a chapter, others a few pages before discussion. At other times the group decided on a time limit and read for ten minutes then talked.

In the group of girls each reading the same Babysitter Club book the predictor, Jenny, was chosen by the teacher because she was not a confident reader and might have had difficulties summarising, questioning or clarifying. Jenny introduced the book to the group, then she asked each person to predict what the story would be about. The group read the first chapter silently after their predictions.
The questioner asked,

'Does this remind you of anything?'

and received the following responses:

Yes, my sister, my brother and I have three different dads. My dad drank too much and the kids had to go to court to say who we would live with.

It reminds me of one of my friends and their experiences.

Once I was kidnapped by my mum's so-called boyfriend when Mum and Dad split up.

READING AND WRITING COMMUNITIES

Roles are introduced and modelled to the class.

It reminds me of my dad's family. They always fight.

My mum and dad hardly ever fight.

It reminds me of my sister and her boyfriend.

The group of children could have discussed this for an hour. The summariser interrupted and said it was time for her summary. Next the clarifier, Pam, asked,

Was there anything you did not understand?

'*Yes!*' said Chelsea, '*What does brunch mean?*' The clarifier didn't know so referred the question to others in the group.

Does anyone else know?

The group decided brunch was a late breakfast. Feedback was given by all students when they returned to the circle. Then Sue asked four children, at random, to report on whether their initial predictions had been accurate. Individual responsibility and accountability was as important as the group responsibility to support each other as readers.

HOME RESPONSE

While they are engaged in these co-operative reading experiences, children are continually monitoring each other's responses to reading

SETTING AND MEETING GOALS: READING

and providing feedback. Goal setting flows naturally from making reading and writing explicit, and from practice and feedback because it is at the feedback point that we say 'OK that's done,' or 'You could try again, maybe trying a different tack, a different strategy such as rereading the sentence if you don't know the word.'

Sue Ryan provides information about achievement of goals to parents in a parent response journal. Lyn also sends home a record of children's reading for parents to add comments. The reading record goes home with the child each day after school.

Please sign, date and comment (if you wish) after reading with your child.

Date	Name of book	Sign/Date	Listener's comments	Lyn' comments
13/9	Bertie & the bear	20/9	Read this book 4 times. He thoroughly enjoyed testing everyone in our house	yes!!!
20/9	Caps for Sale	10/10	Didn't read to me last night	We've got the same favorite part
12/10	Mogs Mumps	14/10	Had problems with long words. Unable to say catastrophe let alone read it	He appears keen and keeps trying great!

How do we as teachers know when we've reached our goals? It helps if the goals are clear and explicit. It helps if we list specific behaviour to observe as outcomes to show that we have achieved our goals.

Goals for co-operative reading described in this chapter included the following:

> Do children appreciate a range of purposes for reading? Do they demonstrate reading for:
> - enjoyment
> - shared experiences
> - information
> - instructions
>
> Do children engage in reading practice?
> - individually
> - partners
> - cross-age tutoring
> - group reading and discussions
>
> Do children have a range of responses to reading?
> - discussing and piggybacking on ideas
> - recognising literary elements and techniques
> - writing and expressing responses in a range of media
> - sharing information about authors and linking literary techniques to other books
>
> Are children improving their reading strategies for understanding and evaluating texts?
> - predicting
> - questioning
> - summarising
> - clarifying
>
> Can children set and assess their own and the group achievement of goals?
> - can individuals set goals for improvement?
> - do groups set goals on how to improve working together?
> - do students take each other's advice, feedback and recommendations seriously?

5
SETTING AND MEETING GOALS: WRITING

At the beginning of term 4 the children in Lyn Thompson's Reception to Year 2 class are deciding which sorts of writing they will try this term. Last term they had all attempted seven different types. The list of these was charted on the wall as well as on a sheet of paper pasted into each child's writing book. When they had attempted a form the children coloured in a dot next to that form, as a record. They could then see the other sorts of writing they could consider next.

Writing range sheet for term 3	
1. Raps and rhymes	0
2. Letter	0
3. Story	0
4. Poster	0
5. Fuzzy card	0
6. Y chart	0
7. Recount	0

The writing range sheet is the focus for the children's writing for the term. It sets out their major writing goals, showing what they are aiming for, what they have already achieved, and what they might work on next. The term's writing program is based on this list. During the term Lyn plans to make explicit and provide for practice in each of the listed types, and with these as her framework, she focuses on particular aspects of the writing process, the various mechanics of writing, and specific ways to make writing effective.

CLASSROOM CLIMATE AND THE WRITING PROGRAM

The goals of the term's writing program are to further students'
- appreciation of the range of writing forms
- use of a range of genres
- skill in using the writing process and mechanics
- effectiveness in writing
- ability to evaluate their own writing.

These goals are co-ordinated with the goals for creating a cohesive co-operative classroom, not only because in such classrooms all children have a chance to learn, but also because language learning is essentially social, and co-operative tasks involve social interaction.

Most language use and language learning depends on at least two people being involved. Writing, like talking, is a form of communi-

Class meetings set a classroom climate for reading and writing.

cation. To be effective, each piece of writing must be shaped by its purpose and intended audience. The writer must therefore know about the audience and be able to predict its reaction to the writing. Young children learn about the effectiveness of writing in classrooms and at home when they see a mother's pleasure at reading *I Luv My MuM*, and when they witness their classmates' squeals of pleasure at a joke another child has written. The classroom climate is therefore particularly important for developing writers. (Graves 1983, Hill 1984, Hansen 1987) Not only must the students want to make the effort to have an effect on their classmates — to want them as their audience — but they must feel secure and supported enough to have their first efforts read by their classmates.

Peers provide information and support.

Teachers have also found that fellow students are invaluable as a source of information and support. (Calkins 1983, Brock 1987) Writing is a complicated skill that involves using knowledge of topics, vocabulary, grammar, spelling, layout and punctuation. Young writers are learning to use all of these simultaneously, and often need on-the-spot assistance or confirmation. 'How do you write a "P" for penguin?' 'Do you have a capital in "uncle"?' 'Does "because" have an "E" on the end?' 'Where do you put the date in a letter?' . . . In co-operative classrooms these questions can be readily solved by other students. The teacher is then free for other teaching.

This chapter sets out basic strategies for achieving the five goals in the writing program. Some, but not all, of the strategies incorporate co-operative methods. Strategies that are not specifically co-operative, such as making expected behaviour explicit, contribute to the cohesive and co-operative climate of the class. Other strategies, such as providing for individual choice, are valuable because of their contribution to individual engagement.

GOALS AND STRATEGIES FOR WRITING

Appreciation of the range of writing forms	Class writing range sheet Student range sheet Class survey Teacher uses range of forms Variety for student choice Teacher uses correct terms
Practice in using a range of genres	Making genres specific Identifying key features Daily practice Specific feedback Writing checker Group conference Pair conferences
Skill using the writing process and conventions	Incidental teaching Teacher think alouds Collaborative composition Response to individual writing Co-operative writing
Effectiveness in writing	Good models Share circles Celebration

SETTING AND MEETING GOALS: WRITING

> Peer and self-evaluation of writing
>
> Demonstrations
> Sharing circles
> Charted suggestions
> Writing contracts

APPRECIATING A RANGE OF FORMS
WRITING RANGE SHEET

'I need your help to make our writing range sheet for this term,' begins Lyn. 'Later you will make a range sheet of your own. We'll have a think-pair-share to come up with all the types of writing we know. First we'll have a think time together. Think of all the different types of writing you could do.'

The children sit silently. Lyn looks thoughtful, concentrating, eyes down. She silently counts off items on her fingers and nods with each finger; she looks up, counts off another few, then looks around the room at the sorts of writing she can see. She seems oblivious of the children, who are quiet, presumably also thinking. They can see what sort of behaviour goes with thinking.

'Have you all had enough time to think of the different types of writing?' She looks around the circle to see if they are nodding and ready.

'Turn to the person next to you for a knee-to-knee.' The children turn to a partner and each pair sits knee-to-knee, crossed-legged. Some children need to shift to find a partner.

'First person,' says Lyn, and one of each pair starts telling the other what they have thought of. Most of the children are making eye contact and nodding as they listen. They know that that is successful behaviour of a knee-to-knee.

'Stories, journal . . . songs. That's all I can think of,' John says to his partner.

'I can hear some people talking. Sharon's talking. Kristie's talking. Benjamin is making eye contact. Rebecca is nodding . . . Second person,' announces Lyn, and the partners swap roles.

After about 90 seconds Lyn tells the group it is time to share and the children swing around into a circle again. Lyn has a long piece of paper headed 'Range of writing', and a marker pen ready to record what the children say. Lyn names a child: 'Georgia, what sort of writing did you think of?'

'Posters,' says Georgia. Lyn nods and writes that on her list. 'Elizabeth?'

'Letter.'

Each child in turn around the circle contributes a type of writing.

Only once is there any repetition. When a response is unclear or is not a type of writing, Lyn prompts for a more appropriate contribution from the contributor or asks the group to help that person. For example, when Tania says, 'Normal,' Lyn says 'I don't know what normal is. What sorts of writing do you know?' Tania takes a while to focus on an answer but eventually says, 'A note.'

When Natasha says, 'Story,' Lyn asks, 'What is the proper name for a story?' Natasha doesn't know so Lyn asks if someone can help her. Four hands go up and Christopher suggests, 'Narrative.'

Mary offers, 'Environment,' and when Lyn asks, 'What sort of writing would that be?' Mary answers, 'A report.'

When Shaun says, 'Something that's happened,' Lyns asks whether she is talking about a report or a recount. Shaun replies, 'A recount. It's something you've done.'

'Can anyone tell Shaun what a report is?' asks Lyn.

It is Sarah who says, 'You write down who, where, when, how.'

When everyone in the circle has had a turn, Lyn asks if there are any other sorts of writing they know. Eventually they have recorded all the types they can think of. There are thirty-five types on the list.

Now that the whole class has helped to produce the range sheet they are ready to select those genres that they will all write this term.

Lyn explains: 'Now that we've got the big picture of the range of writing, we need to go through these and pick out seven for our term's writing range sheet and decide how many of each we will do. You can then decide on three other forms that you want to do.'

The first seven suggestions were ticked and the number that they agreed they would write of each recorded, as well as the number of days they would include in a journal and the TV book. Later Lyn prepared a sheet to paste in each child's writing book, and a large matching chart for the wall for easy reference. The range sheet with the thirty-five genres was also displayed so that each child could select the three to add to his or her own list.

Term 4 writing range sheet

1. Book
2. Song
3. Instructions
4. Personal journal (5 days)
5. Y Chart
6. Raps and rhymes
7. TV guide (5 days)
8.
9.
10.

SETTING AND MEETING GOALS: WRITING

The range sheet is displayed for future use.

Over the year, the children have gradually extended the range of genres they are familiar with. Each term Lyn has negotiated a range sheet with the class and the children have determined which they would practise in that term.

The range sheets provide a broad picture of the variety of ways that writing is used. A class survey, where the children asked their parents to indicate what sorts of reading the child did at home, also raised the children's awareness of the range and purposes of their reading. Other ways of demonstrating the various purposes and types of writing occur throughout each day.

TEACHER USES DIFFERENT GENRES

Every day Lyn reads a variety of genres to her class. On any one day she might read three stories, four notes, six raps or rhymes, three lists, three cards, a Y chart, a letter, an announcement, a lost-and-found notice, an agenda, two songs, three labels and a thank-you note. These might be from parents, other teachers, the principal, from the class book of shared raps and rhymes, or as part of the day's decision making. Lyn takes care to refer to each form of writing by its correct name and incidentally also refers to key features of that form: 'This notice tells us *what* is going to happen, *when* it will be (the day, date and time) and *where* to go.' 'The address on the envelope has street and house number, the suburb is Port Adelaide, and the postcode is also there, in case we need to write back.'

<u>Writing range sheet</u> Term 4

- o book
- oo songs
- o instructions
- o journal/diary
- o Y chart
- o Maths recording
- o rap/rhyme
- o T.V. book (5 pages)
- oo _____
- o _____
- oo _____

My opinions: 21/8/90

Me I'm good at mathe
I really try at
runing fast.
I'ts hard to Make puppets.
I'm happy when I read puff
the Maigic Dragon I'm good at
catting and pasting. I Like when
I go out to play

Things I can do. 2-6-90
I can do reading. I can do
painting. I can do d the weel.
I can do record patteh
I can do braains stooms
I can do raps and rhymes
I can do patterns. I can do a
Friend Ship Book

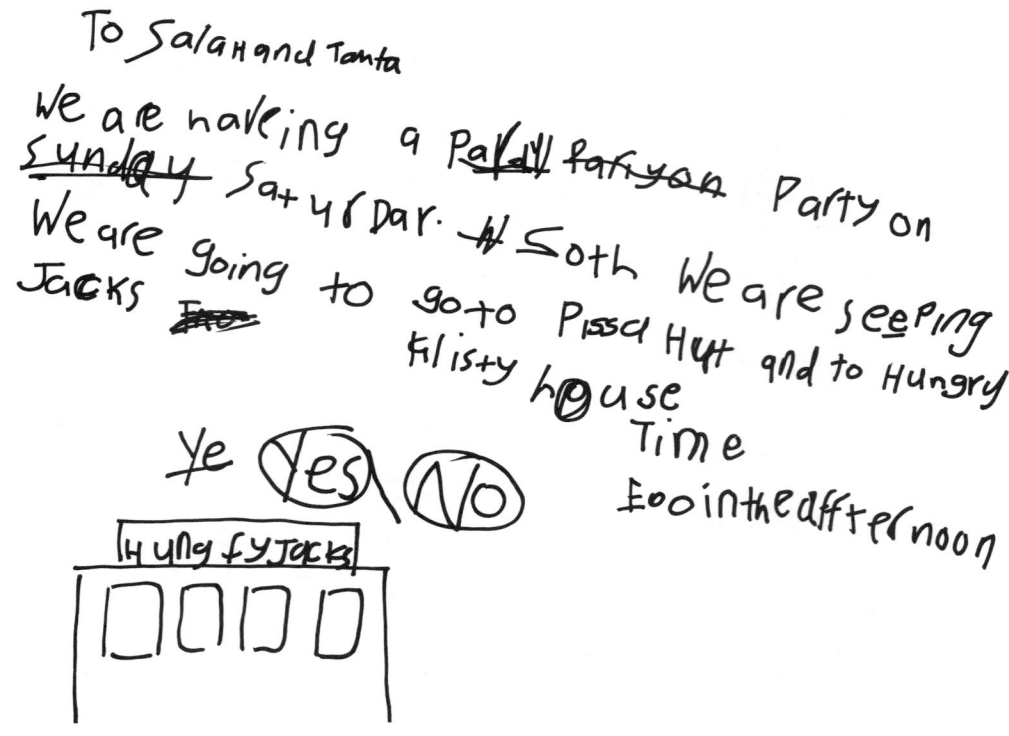

VARIETY OF TEXTS FOR STUDENT CHOICE

There are a variety of genres available for children to read whenever there is free choice reading (at least once a day): cards, catalogues, magazines, comics, non-fiction, poetry, TV guides, the raps and rhymes big book, as well as the usual picture books. Lyn makes sure that examples of the genres that the children have chosen to practise in their writing are always available in the class. She is also careful to have the books organised so that the children can find what they are looking for — reference books are kept in one shelf, books from the school library in another, and books for practising reading are sorted into different coloured boxes according to their difficulty.

TEACHER USES CORRECT TERMS

Lyn takes the opportunity to refer to different types of writing whenever they are used in the class:

> David has written a thank-you note to Mrs Haden who read us that story yesterday.
> There's a report of the school basketball games in the Bulletin.
> If you have made a poster you can pin it to the board next to the clock.

She also points out features of different genres and asks the children about these, sometimes with the large group, sometimes when she is working with one child:

What would you expect to see at the top of a letter?
See how Jenny has written her name in large capitals in the middle of her poster so that people can easily see what it's about.
What do these names on the front of this book tell me?

USING A RANGE OF GENRES

MAKING GENRES EXPLICIT

With the specific genres that the class are going to work on during the term established, the teacher's role is then to make explicit the characteristics of each of the selected genres, and to provide for practice and feedback on the children's efforts in using these genres. There are a variety of ways that a teacher can do this. A combination is best.

Once or twice a week, Lyn takes time to explore the different features of a particular genre with the class. During the term she models each genre that the children have chosen to write during that term, and works with the children to list the common elements.

The essential steps are:
1. The teacher uses and makes available examples of the genre.
2. The class identifies the purposes, audiences and key features of the genre.
3. The class jointly constructs an example of the genre.
4. The children write their own.

IDENTIFYING KEY FEATURES: TV GUIDE

When the class decided to include writing a television guide on their range sheet, Lyn brought along four TV guides for the class to refer to. The class brainstormed for content.

What's on	The time	Talk bubbles
Reviews	Shows	When movies are on
What channel	The date	What movies are comming out.
Crosswords	AO and G	
Posters	Star Wars	Titles

Lyn helped clarify these suggestions:

What do you mean by 'titles'?
Who knows what 'AO' means?
What other codes do they have?
What do you mean 'posters'?
Will I always find 'Star Wars' in a TV guide?

IDENTIFYING KEY FEATURES: TV REVIEW

Then, using one of the TV guides Lyn had in the class as a model, the class composed a review of a television show. First they worked out which show most of them knew about: *Agro's Cartoon Connection*. Lyn then guided the class in identifying the features of a review, providing information as it was needed.

What time and channel is Agro's Cartoon Connection?
We write it in digital time.
Let's have comments about it.
Reviews have comments and opinions.
What happens in the show?
Who is Agro? Can you give me more information about Agro?
Instead of 'cartoons like . . .' you say 'cartoons such as . . .' That's book language.
At no stage in this review (Lyn is reading from a TV guide) does it say 'I like'. How can we say what's best?
Who predominantly are these cartoons for?
Any other information?

The completed review was charted and pinned on the wall for reference.

DAILY PRACTICE

Every day for at least half an hour the children work on the different genres that have been agreed on for the term. At the beginning of the writing time Lyn might introduce a new genre, read an example of a genre, or have a child's writing as the focus for acknowledging the features of a genre — always focusing on what the child has achieved. She then checks that each of the children know what they are going to work on next.

If a child is unsure of what to do Lyn invites the other children to make a suggestion: 'Who can help Andrew work out what he will do this writing time?' Six hands go up.

'You could get your writing book and see if you have made a poster and if you haven't you could get some paper and make one,' suggests Shaun.

When there are children who don't know what their writing will

SETTING AND MEETING GOALS: WRITING

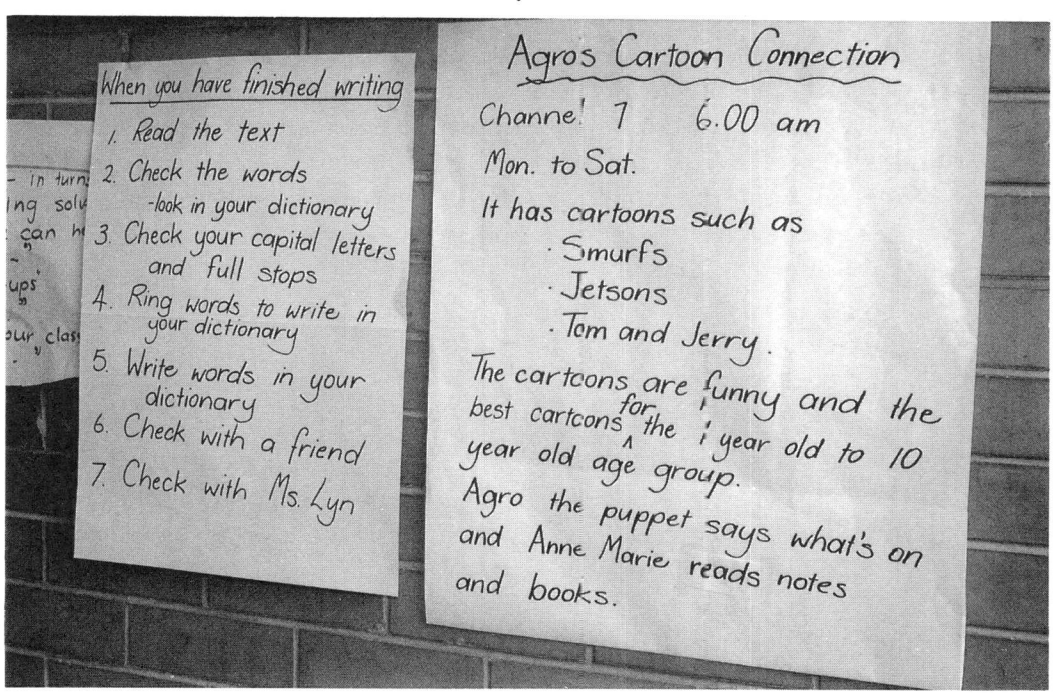

The final TV review was made into a chart displayed for future reference.

be about, Lyn also sets up structures for them to help each other. 'You two form a knee-to-knee and take turns in suggesting some topics.' With more confident children she might say, 'Find someone and ask them to help you brainstorm what you might make a poster about.'

SPECIFIC FEEDBACK

During the writing session Lyn is available to help the writers reflect on what they have done. With beginning writers she will make explicit what they have achieved and guide them in reflecting on what they have done and what they might work on next.

> *I see you have written a story and drawn a picture about it. Tell me what it's about.*
> *Read me your story.*
> *You've introduced your character, 'the mean shark', then you've told me about the terrible things the shark did. And now what are you going to write?*

With more experienced writers, Lyn will put more of the responsibility on the child to explain what has been achieved:

> *Tell me what you have here, Rebecca . . . Tell me what you have included.*

Then if the child needs more prompting she will give it:

> *Is there any other information someone would need to get to the Circus?*
> *Are you happy with your poster?*

WRITING CHECKER

Children can learn to be the checker for all sorts of work — for maths, listening, talking to the class, working co-operatively, spelling, tidying up, using features of a genre, punctuation. As long as the features to be checked have been made explicit, children can learn to take on this role. As with any other role, the teacher needs to help make explicit the role of a checker, using a range of strategies. For a writing checker the role is:

1 Read the list of features
2 Read through the writer's work
3 Tick all the features used
4 Explain to the writer

GROUP CONFERENCE

Like all structures, the teacher needs to make explicit the purpose and procedure of a group conference. The purpose is to share work and receive feedback. The procedure is that the group sits in a circle and gives attention to the writer, who reads aloud the piece of writing and then asks for feedback. In Lyn's class the children know that the invitation for feedback is, 'Any comments or questions?'

Lyn has established, through frequent modelling and acknowledgement of appropriate feedback, that comments can be about anything noticed:

I wrote a story about a robot too. My robot was called Eddie . . .
I thought 'Robbie Robot' was a good name . . .
I liked it when the robot tripped over the cord.

Questions tend to give writers ideas about what else they might include. Occasionally, they provide an opportunity to explain.

How could you make a robot out of old bikes? . . .
Did the robot get broken up when it fell over?

When all children who want to give feedback have done so, the reader finishes by saying what he/she is going to do with the piece of writing — write some more, put it in for 'publishing', draw a picture. It is then the next writer's turn.

Group conferences will often be set up by the teacher during writing time, as different children complete their work or want some help. Sometimes the teacher will set these up as pair conferences. In a class where pair and group conferences are a regular part of the writing session, the children will often initiate an informal conference with someone else:

Will you give me a writing conference on my letter please?

SETTING AND MEETING GOALS: WRITING

Peer conferencing allows children to share work and receive feedback.

ANOTHER GENRE: A POSTER

A similar process was used when the class constructed a poster for the school fête. First the children shared their experieces of posters: they suggested posters for the circus, for films, for singers and for a sale. Then Lyn guided them in the sort of information and layout that they needed to consider.

> *What is the most important information on a poster?*
> *Where shall we put that?*
> *What else do people need to know?*
> *Let's check: Who? What? When? Where? How?*
> *What else do you think the poster needs?*

Lyn is clear about the features that she expects in different forms of writing and reinforces children's knowledge of these in their writing or as the class comes into contact with the different forms:

> *That sounds as though it had a beginning and a problem. What sort of writing is that?*
> *Sarah wrote an invitation and she used a wonderful phrase, 'Come and join us.' I really liked that. It sounded friendly. I'm going to use that in my poster. What other information do we need on an invitation?*
> *If you write a letter what do you put at the top?*

SETTING AND MEETING GOALS: WRITING

ANOTHER GENRE: PERSUASIVE WRITING

Sue Ryan's Year 6 class is learning about presenting an argument. They have discussed the important elements of presenting a position. They know it needs to have
- a brief statement of the position taken
- an introduction to the two sides of an argument
- elaboration of each position
- a conclusion of the preferred position and why

Persuasive Writing

Ryan 6K

"10 pm Curfew In Pt. Augusta

I believe that the 10pm Curfew in Pt. Augusta shouldn't go on.
There are 3 reasons to support my argument.
Firstly, you couldn't go to the phone box.
Secondly, you can't go over your friends house.
Finally, you couldn't go to the shop.
Some people would argue & say that there should be a curfew because of Juvenile crime.
However, I believe they are wrong because it will be your responsibility or fault if you go out after 10pm.

The children have worked for a number of weeks collecting arguments for both sides of the issues and at being able to state both sides. The first issue dealt with was whether or not young people should have a 10 o'clock curfew. The suggestion had been reported as a solution to youth crime in a country town.

Before tackling the issue, the class developed and then revised their rules for arguments through a think-pair-share. They then brainstormed arguments for one side of the argument in small groups. Then they each brainstormed ideas for the other side of the argument, each group member taking a different role: encourager, facilitator, recorder and presenter. Those roles where also useful when groups distinguished between arguments that were fact and arguments that were opinion. Then in pairs in a knee-to-knee they took turns to present both sides of the argument.

Finally two children, taking opposite sides to the argument, were asked to reach agreement in a fishbowl, so that the class could observe and then discuss the alternative ways that agreement could be reached.

The children identified with the young people in the country town and readily found arguments against the curfew. They also had no difficulty in coming up with counter arguments. Other issues that Sue found equally engaging were also current at the time:

- Whether or not Ninja Turtles should be banned.
- Whether Year 7 should be at the high or the primary school.

After brainstorming sessions for each side, and observations of pairs of children presenting and listening to the two sides of an argument (fishbowl) the children decided which side they favoured and were

---

PERSUASIVE WRITING   Name _____

Topic:

I believe that:

There are ____ reasons to support my argument.
Firstly,

Secondly,

Finally,

Some people would argue that

However, I believe that they are wrong because

provided with the format of sentence beginnings for presenting a persuasive argument.

Each student completed a persuasive writing sheet for the argument and these were compiled in a book so that everyone could read each other's positions. After working with the set format on three topics, the children presented their written arguments without the aid of the sentence beginnings.

PERSUASIVE WRITING NAME: Dona
TOPIC: Yr 7 going to High School

* I believe that the Year 7 students shouldn't go to High School

* There are **3** reasons to support my argument.
1 Firstly, because It would cost the parents too much money for their books and things

2 Secondly, because more younger children will be exposed to drugs

Finally, because there will be more pressure on the students

* Some people would argue that and say Year 7 students should go to High School because it would be better for their education and they might get to like school and stay there longer

* However, I believe they are wrong because I don't think that it would make them stay at school longer.

SKILLS IN USING THE WRITING PROCESS AND CONVENTIONS

The third major set of goals in teaching writing is to understand and use the process and conventions (or mechanics) of writing. The understandings can be grouped as follows:

Process of writing
- We need ideas and information for writing
- First thoughts are written in a rough draft
- Writing for others generally needs revision
- Other people can provide helpful feedback
- Final copies need careful proofreading

Concepts of print
- Writing is left to right, top to bottom
- Words are made up of letters with consistent shapes
- We can write what we say and then read it back

Spelling
- People can usually decipher unconventional spelling
- There are agreed ways of spelling words
- Unconventional spelling distracts the reader
- Correct spelling makes reading easier
- Dictionaries provide correct spelling

Punctuation
- Punctuation signals different things to the reader
- Correct punctuation makes texts easier to read

Written English
- Complete sentences are expected in written texts
- In writing we generally use more formal forms of expression

Learning about the process and these conventions and how to use them are part of every writing program and a part of using any written genre. There are a number of ways that students can support each other in learning to use these conventions and these can be taught incidentally as a part of using print.

INCIDENTAL TEACHING

The class have been singing and chanting raps and rhymes. They have been nodding, jigging, clicking and clapping with the rhythms and the actions. They have just finished chanting 'Parcel in the post'. Lyn asks, 'Who thinks they could find a word here with an apostrophe?' Simon is chosen from the hands that are raised and he points to *said*. Lyn says, 'Close,' then asks 'Who else?' Jane points to *He'd* and Lyn writes on the board *He would*. The class helps Lyn to locate *it's* and *can't*. Lyn explains that a part is left out and an apostrophe put in its place.

Lyn uses this diversion from the fun of raps and rhymes to identify other forms of punctuation. 'Who thinks they could find a comma? Alisha used a comma yesterday in her writing.' 'A question mark?' When these have been identified Lyn concludes, 'You can now check for apostrophes.'

The next song is 'You can't ride a bike in a buffalo herd'. The class sings four verses with their usual enthusiasm and afterwards Lyn asks whether they saw any apostrophes. The class contributes and they clarify what the abbreviated forms stand for. Then there are two more rhymes without any discussion.

Most raps and rhymes sessions will have no reference at all to aspects of the text. The emphasis is on pleasure from print. Lyn is judicious about any focus away from that pleasure. But she is also ready to pick the right time to point out interesting aspects of conventions in the various written pieces that the class shares:

Cathy Timms spells her name in a different way from Kathy Smith.
David has finished his letter with a full stop.
I can tell when the mother speaks because Jenny has used quotation marks.
See how on the news sheet Mrs G has put a row of dots. What do you think she means by that?

TEACHER THINK ALOUDS

Every time a teacher writes in front of students there is an opportunity to reveal the many decisions a writer makes. Teachers often invite the students to suggest what needs to be considered. The teacher may be working with one child, with a group or with the whole class. Teachers choose what it is they want to make explicit according to the writing skills of the students.

When writing a list using the children's suggestions Lyn might say:

This is a list so I use a long piece of paper.
I start writing at the top.
The list is about 'Things that are curved' so I'll write that at the top.
I'll begin with a capital because it's a heading.
'Things' begins with a 'th'. What letters are in 'th'?
How could I show that it's a heading?
Now I'll write one after the other on different lines because it's a . . .?

Lyn is careful that this commentary and invitations to make suggestions do not interfere with the main focus of the writing.

Think alouds are also valuable for making explicit the different parts of the writing process as Chris McLeod (1990) shows in collaborative composition with her class.

READING AND WRITING COMMUNITIES

COLLABORATIVE COMPOSITION

There are numerous forms of writing that lend themselves to collaborative composition where the teacher demonstrates, clarifies special features, asks for assistance, alternatives and justification of preferences, and ends up with a model that can be displayed for the students' own reference.

Whatever the form, the teacher can demonstrate how to deal with the mechanics of writing and reveal aspects of the writing process.

Process:
On Friday night I panicked because I couldn't find my car and I thought that would be a great idea for a story.
I got my ideas down as fast as I could. I didn't worry about my spelling.
Can I read you my story so far so you can tell me if it's clear?

Punctuation:
This is the beginning of a sentence so I use a capital letter.
I'll read it through to see if that's the end of a sentence. If it's the end of a complete thought I'll put a . . .? [full stop]
This list is in a sentence so I put a comma between each item.
I'll use full stops between the numbers in the date.
Someone is speaking so I use quotation marks at the beginning and to show where the speaking stops.
The hat belongs to Jenny so I'll put in an apostrophe. How can we work out where to put the apostrophe?

Spelling:
'She' begins with a 'sh'. What letters are in 'sh'?
'Different' is a long word so I'll need to break it up: 'diff-er-ent'.
Now what are all the sounds in 'actually'? 'ac-tu-al-ly.' [says aloud then writes each syllable as it's said]
I'm not sure whether 'arguments' has an 'e' in it or not. I'll write both on a scrap of paper and see which looks right. [writes] *What do you think?*
I'm still not sure which it is, how can I check? [Find it on a chart or look it up in a dictionary]
That's a word I'm going to have to learn. I'll write it on my word card.

Formatting:
It's the beginning of a story so I'll indent.
I'll show where my paragraphs begin by leaving a line between each. Then I won't need to indent.
This is my heading so I'll write it in the middle at the top and underline.
I need to show that this is a new verse, so I'll leave a blank line.
I'll need to make the event stand out on the poster, how can I do that?
Let's look at some other examples of posters to see how I can do that.

RESPONSE TO INDIVIDUAL WRITING

Teachers make the same sort of commentary to confirm a writer's mastery of different strategies, the various mechanics in their own writing, and to introduce them to mechanics that they are ready to consider. It is important that the comments on the mechanics are few and do not take precedence over the teacher's reactions to the message in the writing.

> *You've used a capital letter at the beginning because it's the beginning of a sentence. And I can see the end of a sentence; there's a full stop.*
> *You've got a new thought here, how will you show the reader?*
> *You've changed the order here, to make it clearer.*
> *There are some words that need to be checked for their spelling. See if you can find which . . . How will you work out the correct spelling?*

CO-OPERATIVE WRITING

When children work in pairs or as a group to produce a single piece of writing, it is a form of co-operative problem solving. As long as the group or pair wants to reach a similar goal, the writing focuses attention and provides the motivation for finding ways to work together.

A teacher can structure for co-operative writing by having groups work on a puppet play, a collection of poems, riddles, book reviews, comic writing, author studies or short stories. The teacher can ensure

Responding to individual writing is an important part of the process.

that all children feel they can make a contribution by recognising expertise in the various aspects of writing such as coming up with ideas, finding the right word, suggesting interesting and unusual words, spelling, framing well-formed, lyrical sentences, responding to drafts, reading out loud, illustrating, finding other ways of saying something, using punctuation, decorating covers, proofreading and presentation.

The teacher can further encourage group interdependence by making the group accountable for each member having a role in producing the final piece. This can be done by identifying roles that need to be allocated, such as writer, reader, illustrator and proofreader, and providing checklists and time to reflect on the contribution of each member.

	Group checklist			
	Contributed ideas	Encouraged	Stayed on task	Acknowledged others' ideas
David Mary				

EFFECTIVENESS IN WRITING

Effectiveness in writing comes with
- experiences of good models of writing
- becoming aware of the features that make the models effective
- wanting to improve the writing
- believing that each writer can improve
- time and strategies for making the necessary changes

Already built into this writing program are structures and practices that provide these conditions:

- Good models and a variety of examples of particular genres are carefully chosen when a new genre is introduced, and when an example of a type of writing is used incidentally in the class the teacher refers to it by its appropriate name. The books provided for the children's reading in the class are also carefully chosen to include a wide range and to be good models. The teacher recognises the importance of reading aloud often to the children and making the reading engaging by the choice of what is read as well as the way it is read.

- The children become aware of the features of writing that make them effective, partly through the range sheet that ensures that various genres are introduced over each term. The three-step procedure to make explicit and provide for feedback and practice makes clear the essential features and also raises awareness of aspects that make one

SETTING AND MEETING GOALS: WRITING

Where there is an established pattern of positive feedback, children can respond to each other's writing.

instance more effective than another. Teachers have found that share circles, where writers present their work, and also displays, provide a range of models from which students can identify aspects that make one piece more effective than others. By taking care to give specific feedback that identifies a range of significant features, the teacher can set the pattern of what features to look for and to comment on.

> *Travis begins his story with a sentence that really makes me want to read on.*
> *Listen to the sound of the words Tracy uses: 'left behind a cold and crumbling wall'.*
> *Don't you like the title of this poem? 'Hip hip hooray'.*

In classrooms where the teacher has established the positive pattern of specific feedback, children can work in pairs and small groups to take turns in responding to each other's writing.

- Children will have to want to improve if they are going to make the effort required to read over, make revisions, rewrite neatly, proofread and illustrate their work. In classrooms where students make this effort, there is a pride in each other's work, a readiness to respond enthusiastically to their classmates' efforts and a general feeling of mutual appreciation. These students value each other as readers and responders; the students write for each other's interest

READING AND WRITING COMMUNITIES

A writer needs an audience.

and response. Class celebrations of each child's achievements, shared pleasures and rituals, and established patterns of helping each other all contribute to class cohesion.

A ritual established in Judy Smith's class was for the children to decide how many 'hoorays' the class would give a student who had achieved something significant, and then proceed to give them. The day Tracy stayed on task for the whole writing session, she received five 'hoorays'. Tracy had a pattern of walking around the class or being distracted by other children's activities in writing time.

- Children will only make the effort required for writing (and reading) if they believe that they will be successful. Teachers often find that convincing their students that they can succeed is the first priority in their literacy program (Hancock 1991). In classrooms where cohesion and co-operative skills are being developed, the supportive environment, the specificity of what is required, and constant reminders of what is 'successful behaviour' make it possible for every child to have success.

Each child states their individual goals at the beginning of a writing session. The evaluation circle at the end, where each child states to what extent they met their goals, allows for individual differences, the development of realistic goal setting, and an opportunity to reward the class if all achieve their goals. The reward encourages each child to support the others in achieving their goals.

- Time and strategies for revising writing are part of the teacher's program. Ways of revising are easily demonstrated in collaborative writing. Children can be taught how to read over a piece of writing, identify parts that are unclear, clumsy or unnecessary, as well as those that are concise, well stated and informative. They then learn how to come up with alternatives, make judgements and add or delete. All these techniques can be modelled with the whole class and often individually in writing conferences. The teacher can also make clear the expectation that there will be drafts, revisions and rewriting and provide time and support for these, particularly for young children. Many teachers arrange for a parent or a teacher aide to occasionally relieve children of the rewriting chore by typing final drafts. Other teachers reduce the rewriting tedium by building into their program opportunities to draft, revise and correct on a word processor.

A useful strategy in a co-operative classroom is to identify a 'writing conference corner', a 'proofreading corner' and a 'publishing corner' where children can find appropriate materials as well as relevant ideas and assistance from other children who are at the same stage in their writing. Going to these corners signals discussion time; writers in other parts of the room can expect to continue uninterrupted.

An item that is often raised in class meetings in democratic co-operative classrooms is the problem that some children have of being continually interrupted to provide assistance. Through the class meeting, the whole class comes to appreciate the problem and work out solutions.

PEER AND SELF-EVALUATION OF WRITING

All the guidance, commentary, models and feedback that are given in class are directed towards each child becoming independent as a writer: having the confidence to express themselves in writing, knowing which form of writing to use, being able to use the mechanics that are needed, and, finally, being able to judge whether their own writing is likely to achieve the purpose for which it was intended.

Even beginning writers can be encouraged to make judgements about their writing and about each other's writing. The teacher uses writing demonstrations, sharing circles and individual conferences to help children to be explicit about what they like and what they think needs improving, and to become aware of different ways to improve a piece of writing.

DEMONSTRATIONS

In writing demonstrations the teacher can make explicit the choice points and criteria used at different stages of the writing:

> *Let me think, what shall I write about? I could write about going to my nephew's birthday party . . . or yesterday when I left my shopping at the chemist's . . . or the crazy things my dog does . . . Which topic could I make the most interesting? . . . I'll write about leaving the parcel. I had such a panic!*
>
> *I've left a space here because I'm not sure which word is best. I want a word that tells how worried I was, and how flushed I was as well? Can you make any suggestions?*
>
> *I've read through my story and I don't like the beginning. I don't think readers will think it's going to be very interesting. This is what I wrote . . .*

SHARING CIRCLES

In sharing circles the children are invited to give feedback to writing in progress and to finished pieces: 'Is there any feedback that you would like to give Sharon?' Or with the invitation that many classes use: 'Are

The results from sharing feedback co-operatively are charted for all to refer to.

SETTING AND MEETING GOALS: WRITING

there any comments or questions?' Children readily pick up the focuses and the terminology that the teacher has used:

I thought the title sounded interesting.
I liked the words 'roly poly puppy'.
You didn't say what happened when you dropped the lollies.
I thought it was good when you 'skidded to a stop'. That sounded exciting.
I wanted to know more about what you played at the party.

After several weeks of writing demonstrations and responses, the class will be ready to suggest ways of improving a piece of writing, and can be placed in co-operative writing groups, each having responsibility to provide feedback to the others in the group. Brainstormed suggestions for improvement can be charted and pinned up for ready reference.

CHARTED SUGGESTIONS

For successful story writing

List topics and choose one.

Ask someone to suggest a topic.

Get the ideas down quickly.

Read through the story and see if it flows.

Add bits to make it interesting and clear.

Make sure the beginning is interesting.

Is the story rounded off?

Read it to a partner and ask for comments and suggestions.

Check spelling and punctuation.

Write it neatly and in an interesting way.

READING AND WRITING COMMUNITIES

WRITING CONTRACTS

Once the children are used to making judgements and suggestions about writing, they are ready to set their own goals about how they will improve their writing. On their writing contract each child, at the beginning of term, can identify not only the forms of writing they will use, but one or two aspects of their writing that they negotiate with the teacher to work on.

TERM 2 WRITING CONTRACT

Name: Gavin

Student to have 9 final pieces in folio, including at least one of the following. Special care to be taken in these pieces with the aspects identified

Types of writing:	Self evaluation	Teacher evaluation
1. Narrative (tall story) *Story based on The Hoop Snake The Giant Kangaroo*	I thought my story was funny! It built up to the end.	The class and I clearly loved this Gavin! It was great. S.M.
2. Poem *Night*	My first try at a poem without a rhyme. It was hard.	I felt the quiet creepiness of the darkness. Interesting format. S.M.
3. Report *Sportsday Report*	I liked using the headings But I needed more detail from the day.	
4. Letter requesting information		
5. Letter to the Editor		
6. Persuasive argument		
7.		
8.		
9.		

Conventions: paragraphs, punctuation, capitals, sentence structure
I aim to get my paragraphs right and use different size sentences.

Writing process: pre-writing, revision, conferencing, proofreading,
I need to proofread more carefully.

Presentation: handwriting, a new form of publishing
I want to a use cursive more. I'll need to practice.

At the end of each term the class reviews their writing over that period and decides whether they have achieved their goal, and identifies any aspects that they think they did particularly well in preparation for setting their goals at the beginning of the next term. Children can be paired to support each other in reaching their stated goals. In their pairs they can spell out what they will need to do in the short term to achieve their goals, and give feedback to each other after each writing session on what they achieved towards their goal in that session. The teacher can structure for this type of interdependence with different sized groups as well as for pairs, being careful that the children learn to expect to be grouped with any children in the class.

My Writing . . . .

I do like writing stories especially stories about things I make up about me — getting lost and being followed. Sometimes they get very long and I don't know how to finish them. I feel good when I've finished a long story but I'd rather go on to another story than check it for spelling and fix it up. It would be good if I could use a computer for my stories then it would be easy to fix them up.

I want to try more poetry writing next term. I liked the ones that Anna wrote.

6
Reflections on Building Communities of Readers and Writers

♦

A community of readers and writers is a group of people who value reading and writing, who use it constantly for a range of purposes, and where the members of the group help each other to be successful.

The democratic classrooms described in this book show how children and teachers jointly create a world inside the classroom where reading and writing allow them to make connections, communicate ideas, reach out to influence others and achieve satisfaction and enjoyment through literacy experiences.

The teachers play a powerful role demonstrating how they value reading and writing as ways of learning and communicating. Teachers who award literacy a high profile talk about books, read books, share their own reading and writing and value the literacy experiences of the class members; and the students begin to see that through reading and writing they can relate to the teacher and relate to each other. Books allow children to make connnections with each other. After all, it is literature both commercially produced and produced by the class members that makes it possible to talk about personal things in a way that is once removed from one's own experiences.

REFLECTIONS

The communities of readers and writers described here had common features. In each class teachers made explicit what is learnt and how students can work together. Co-operative learning was used to maximise learning and to increase equity and participation of all classroom members. There were common class goals, whole school goals and a strong sense of community between the teachers. The teachers played a proactive role creating forward-looking learning experiences involving both spoken and written communication skills.

MAKING EXPLICIT THE 'WHAT' AND THE 'HOW' OF A LITERACY CULTURE

Building communities of readers and writers involves developing a common language and experiences to define **what** is learned and **how** to work together. The literacy strategies needed to become a reader and writer are demonstrated and the teachers also made explicit various ways of working together. Children learned to take turns, build on each other's responses and take the feedback comments of their peers seriously.

The ways in which we communicate verbally and non-verbally become a focus. It is impossible to separate talking and listening from reading and writing in a literacy community. Children respond to each other's writing, provide ideas when they are needed, listen to each other's predictions for a story, brainstorm arguments for persuasive writing and discuss their written responses about how a character may have changed in a novel. When children acknowledge and value the feedback from their peers, this increases the responsibility of all class members to provide positive, specific and relevant feedback. In comparison, in competitive classrooms children only take what the teacher says seriously and disregard their peers' suggestions.

In co-operative classrooms the literacy activities are structured so that pairs and small groups are interdependent. Class members rely on each other. They need each other. Their comments count. The class members interact more thoughtfully. Children are suddenly valuing the other potential teachers in the class — their peers. Learning how to trust each other, and rely on each other to give support and feedback becomes an explicit part of the classroom experience. The teachers set aside time for feedback on how the group worked, how the members encouraged each other, and for discussing responsibilities as individual group members.

Learning to work together is not concerned with learning good manners or becoming compliant. Working together is about tolerance, consideration, expressing differences, ways to solve problems, and, particularly, how to manage conflict as ideas are challenged, disputed and modified.

CO-OPERATING NOT COMPETING

There are times when children want to work alone, times to withdraw, and times to work in teams in competition with others. Traditional individualised literacy programs have a competitive flavour where children race to write more, read more and bigger books and go on to the next reading group, often at the expense of others and quality of product. Competition in schools will continue in team games and contests. Readjusting with a balance of co-operative activities, however, promotes improved learning. When reading and writing experiences are based on positive interdependence, students care about their peers' successes and achievements and support, challenge and monitor each other's learning. Groups have a co-operative spirit, as all must succeed for the group to succeed.

The teachers in this book avoided using competitive language, 'Is Fred a better reader than Dan? Who can come up with the longest list? Who can get the most books read? Which is the better piece of writing? Who's going to be first to finish their work?' We cannot ignore the fact that competition exists, but competition is not the only way, nor the best way to motivate children. Using competitive language may support those who are first to get their work done. In a competitive situation the winner wins at the expense of others. Can all children remain positive about their efforts if one or two are winning? Research shows us that they don't. In fact, those students who consistently compare unfavourably in competitive classrooms learn to reject the school's values. (Broadfoot 1979)

BUILDING COMMUNITIES TO MAXIMISE LITERACY LEARNING

Co-operative learning strategies are important for maximising children's learning. Children are challenged by their peers. They must justify their opinions, and elaborate and substantiate ideas when working with others. In reading and writing, where ideas are interpreted, expressed and extended, students achieve more, the quality of performance is increased, more critical thinking occurs and facts and information are retained.

> *The more conceptual the task, the more problem solving that is required, the more creative the answers need to be, the greater the superiority of co-operative over competitive or individualistic learning.* (Johnson and Johnson 1990b)

BUILDING COMMUNITIES FOR GREATER EQUITY

When children in Lyn Thompson's class choose to work in friendship groups the most articulate gathered together and the less confident readers tend to end up together in homogeneous groups. It was the case of the language rich getting richer! Lyn used co-operative structures so that all children had to work together and support each other: girls work with boys, Aboriginal and Cambodian children solve problems together, the gifted child works with a class member with learning difficulties. Making successful literacy behaviours explicit, plus structuring so children have to work together, increases participation levels which, in turn, makes for greater equity of learning within the classroom.

In Lyn's classroom all children have rights and responsibilities. They work and behave in ways where all members are supported. This means that there are common procedures and a common language. For all children to access the mainstream culture, this culture is made explicit. There were few fuzzy, grey areas, no soft options, and no hidden procedures which meant children were never unsure or perplexed about what was necessary for success.

BEING PROACTIVE IN TIMES OF CHANGE

At Taperoo Primary School the teachers took a proactive stand to teach children how to manage conflict both in and outside school, how to communicate, run meetings, negotiate and manage their lives. The children were taking these skills home to their parents. It was powerful: powerful for the children and the community outside the school. The children were in no way homogenised, nor had their individual differences been subjugated entirely to meet the requirements of the group. Rather, there was a feeling of acceptance of individuals. There was acceptance of the notion that you are free to be other than 'me' but there were group co-operative values and ways of behaving that all shared.

Changing family patterns and the economic situation may be having an effect on children's learning. It is easy to overgeneralise and say the affluent schools are fine and poor schools are in trouble. Not all children in affluent, advantaged schools are aware of what to do to succeed in the classroom. Although it seems that literacy rich home environments are often linked to economic advantage we must be cautious of these generalisations. A single parent borrowing books from the library may, in fact, spend more time talking about books than a busy family with both parents in full-time work. There is, however, little doubt that the intergenerational poverty of many families in homes around Taperoo and other disadvantaged schools presents particular problems associated with despair, weariness and apathy associated with long-term unemployment and poverty.

Past educational outcomes have been so concerned with content outcomes alone that students may leave school with a good mark but without strategies that will help them communicate and get on with others. Where are students learning how to listen and take each other seriously? In some families this may be a focus but there is enough evidence from the hours spent in front of TV and the fact that parents have to work so hard now to make ends meet that there may be a socialisation void in some families where how to get on with others, how to talk, how to take turns, how to deal with differences, how to listen to others is not part of what is learnt. In addition, family behaviour patterns used to manage conflict may be effective at home but not in a classroom with thirty other children.

BUILDING COMMUNITIES WHERE ALL MEMBERS BELONG

The children in these classrooms were members of a cohesive group. They felt responsible for their efforts when working with their partner or group. The idea that each person belonged to the class was continually stated by the teacher. Their positive efforts were noticed and positive feedback was given. When something went wrong, as it often did, the group worked out strategies or suggestions to get it right. So many learning experiences were based on the idea that we sink or swim together that all felt that their contribution was valued. Only when individual differences are acknowledged and celebrated do the children feel they belong and feel secure in a group.

SHARED GOALS

The teachers in this book maintain that the culture emerges as members build a shared vision or picture of what key ideas or information can be learned together. This shared vision may begin with brainstorming all the different genres of writing used in the classroom and outside in the community. From this list, the teacher selects genres to teach and make explicit. The children select additional forms to learn as individuals. The selection of what to learn easily translates to classroom and individual goals for learning. There are shared goals and specific individual goals.

IMPLICATIONS FOR THE WHOLE SCHOOL

Small communities are powerful in individual classrooms but when there is a whole school united in its efforts to build a shared vision for literacy learning several benefits follow:
- The school has common goals where each class belongs and is part of a unified vision.

REFLECTIONS

When individual differences are acknowledged and celebrated, children feel that they belong and are secure in the group.

- Because all sense they belong, teachers are valued for their different strengths. One does not disappear into a group but rather grows and is celebrated as an individual who is different.
- Staff support each other and there is a net of colleagues ready to encourage risk takers trying new ideas and better ways of learning.
- Because specialist teacher, parents and others associated with the school have a shared vision, common goals and a sense of belonging the librarian, special education teacher, parents and friends enter the school and classroom community as members not fringe dwellers. There is little opportunity to sit on the outside nor is there opportunity to walk in and take over. The community is shaped as each member participates.

BUILDING COMMUNITIES BETWEEN TEACHERS

Teachers who are working in co-operative reading and writing classrooms need support. It is easy to slip back into exclusively competitive ways of teaching and we must continually renew our commitment to working co-operatively to avoid slipping back. Lyn

Thompson and Sue Ryan benefited from the whole school working in a co-operative direction.

The teachers at Taperoo were, most of the time, able to maintain a positive framework for their work because the whole staff continued to refresh and renew their commitment to co-operative learning. Continually reflecting on the ways they work together co-operatively was the linchpin in the success of co-operative learning in reading and writing. Keeping themselves renewed, open and watchful for ways to improve was critical. It was feedback and support from others that enabled them to maintain and improve classroom strategies.

It is the culture — the relationships, the shared values and beliefs, the communication processes, the rituals and ceremonies, the shared language and meanings, the structures and conditions — that must be changed if schools are to achieve real success in educating all children.
(Polly Eckert 1991)

BUILDING COMMUNITIES FOR THE FUTURE

We are in a period of rapid change at the forefront of the post-industrial era (Lankshear 1990). There are economic changes, and changes in family employment patterns with increased employment pressures for some and unemployment for others. Many researchers into family socialisation patterns claim there is a socialisation void for many primary school children. (Johnson and Johnson 1990)

For many of us, academic competition and growth at all costs is not enough any more. Building a more caring environment in our school communities is making sense. We have de-emphasised the importance of social support in education for fifteen years or more. To meet the challenges that lie ahead we must plan for more caring and committed relationships amongst students to increase the support students have for each other. In times of change and with pressure to perform, to learn and solve shared problems, there is need for a match between achievement and the level of social support.

We are aware that in the next twenty years fifty per cent of all job categories will change. Positions such as postal officer may remain but the responsibilities will change totally. Skills needed in the workplace will have to be flexible because current patterns of employment will continue to change.

The literacy skills for the future will be tightly linked with talking and listening. These language skills will involve problem solving, evaluating performance, managing differences, thinking, planning and co-operating. Whenever teachers and students face increased demands

REFLECTIONS

to improve literacy performance, a corresponding emphasis on social support should be structured.

For Lyn Thompson and others in this book, learning to build a cohesive literacy community in a time of social change is critical for their professional development. What is happening in the homes of the children in the class is outside their teaching brief. What they *can* work on is building a safe, secure learning community for students where all can gain access to the literacy and co-operative skills needed to operate effectively in their world. They continue to inspire us.

Building a safe, secure learning community for students.

REFERENCES

Aronson, E., Blaney, N., Stephan, C., Sikes, J. & Snapp, M. 1977, *The Jigsaw Classroom*, Sage Publications, Beverly Hills, Calif.

Atwell, N. 1987, *In the Middle*, Heinemann, Portsmouth, New Hampshire.

Bloom, B. 1956, *Taxonomy of Educational Objectives. Handbook 1: Cognitive Domain*, David MacKay, New York.

Brock, S. 1987, 'Talk helps young writers', *Australian Journal of Reading*, vol. 10, no. 2, pp. 100-109.

Broadfoot, P. 1979, 'Communication in the classroom. A study of the role of assessment in motivation. *Educational Research*, 31, Fall, pp. 3-10.

Calkins, L. 1983, *Lessons from a Child*, Heinemann, Portsmouth, New Hampshire.

Calkins, L. 1987, *The Art of Teaching Writing*, Heinemann, Portsmouth, New Hampshire.

de Bono E. 1991, *Handbook for the Positive Revolution*, Viking, London.

Dishon D. and Wilson, P. 1991, 'It looks easier than it is', *Co-operative Learning Magazine*, vol. 11, no. 3. pp. 45-6.

Eckert, P. 1991, 'Preparing for the 21st Century by collaborative learning for a happier and more productive school', *Primary Focus*, Education Department of South Australia.

Gardner, H. 1991, *The Unschooled Mind*, Basic Books, USA.

Graves, D. 1983, *Writing: Teachers and Children at Work*, Heinemann, Portsmouth, New Hampshire.

Graves, N. and Graves, T. 1990, *A Part to Play: Tips, Techniques and Tools for Learning*, Latitude Media, Melbourne.

Hancock, J. 1991, 'Priorities in teaching reading', *English Language Newsletter*, no. 1.

Hancock, J. 1989, 'Extending responses to reading in the classroom using literature logs,' Paper presented at the Australian Reading Association and AATE National Conference, Darwin.

Hansen, J. 1987, *When Writers Read*, Heinemann, Portsmouth, New Hampshire.

Hill, S. and Hill, T. 1990, *The Collaborative Classroom*, Eleanor Curtain Publishing, Melbourne.

Hill, K. 1984, *The Writing Process*, Nelson, Melbourne.

Johnson, R. and Johnson, D. 1989, *Co-operation and Competition: Theory and Research*, Interaction Book Company, Edina, MN.

Johnson, R. and Johnson, D. 1990a, 'What is co-operative learning?', in *Perspectives on Small Group Learning; Theory and Practice*, eds M. Brubacher, P. Ryder and R. Kemp, Rubicon Publishing, Ontario.

REFERENCES

Johnson, D. and Johnson, R. 1990b, 'Co-operative learning and achievement', in *Co-operative Learning: Theory and Research*, ed. S. Schlomo, Praeger, New York.

Kagan, S. 1990, *Co-operative Learning: Resources for Teachers*, San Juan, Capistrano, CA. 1982.

Lankshear, C. 1991, 'Getting it right is hard: Redressing the politics of literacy in the 1990s', *16th Australian Reading Association Selected Papers*, Australian Reading Association, Adelaide.

McLeod, C. 1990, 'Children help a teacher to write,' in *Successful Stories from the Classroom*, vol. 1, eds L. Badger, P. Cormack and J. Hancock, PETA, Sydney.

Palincsar, A.S., and Brown, A.L. 1986, 'Interactive teaching to promote independent learning from text,' *The Reading Teacher*, vol. 39, no. 8, pp. 771-7.

Raphael, T. E., et al. 1992, 'Research directions: Literature and discussion in the reading program', *Language Arts*, vol. 69, no. 1, pp. 54-61.

Topping, K. 1989, 'Peer tutoring and paired reading: Combining two powerful techniques', *The Reading Teacher*, vol. 47, no. 7, pp. 488-94.

INDEX

acceptable behaviours 41
assessment *see* evaluation

big picture/small picture 57
book discussions 80–1
bookshares 77–8

chairperson's script 6, 14
change in the broader community 125–6
charting feedback 119
choosing partners 42
choral reading 63
class meetings 5–6
class rules 34
classroom cultures 29–30
  teacher's role 1–2
  strategies for establishing acceptable behaviours 34–41
cohesion 31
  and trust 39–41
  strategies for developing 31–41
cohesive cultures 30–41
collaborative composition 112
communication skills 59
concepts of print 110
conventions (mechanics) of writing 110–14
co-operation vs. competition 124
co-operative classrooms 123
  structures 9–10
co-operative learning 43–4
  benefits for literacy learning 58–61
co-operative reading
  goals and strategies 64–7, 90
co-operative skills 43
  feedback 48–9
  list of 45
  making explicit 46–9
  practising 46–8
co-operative structures 49–58

co-operative writing 113
co-operative vs. traditional
  groups 50
  structures 60, 124
criteria for a happy day 13
cross-age tutoring 70–1

demonstrations, writing 118
displays of print 10–22

EEKK 55
effective learning 41
equity in the literacy classroom 124–5
evaluation
  reading 86–90
  writing 117–21
exchange reading 71–2
explicit teaching
  checking role 104
  class culture behaviours 30, 31
  co-operative learning 123
  co-operative skills 44, 46–9
  group conferences 104
  literacy strategies 123
  reading for pleasure 28
  responsibility 38
  roles 7
  stages of writing 118
  writing conventions 111

feedback 48–9
  from peers 123
  on writing 103
  quick ideas 49
  recording on charts 119
formatting 112
friendship groups 53

genres
  identifying key features 101–2
  making explicit 101

posters 105–6
reading a variety aloud 97–100
TV guides 101–2
TV reviews 102
using a range for writing 101–109
using the correct language 100–1
variety for student choice 100
see also writing forms
goal interdependence 50
goals 36–7
group cohesion 30–1
group conferences 104
group interdependence 114
group readings 62–3
group responsibility 38–9
grouping, structuring for co-operation 60–1

home literacy communities 9
huddle 56

incidental teaching, writing conventions 110–11
individual responsibility 38–9
interdependence 50–2, 114, 123

jigsaw 57–8

knee-to-knee 55, 95, 100

language of writing 100–1
literacy demands for the future 127–8
literacy
   activities in co-operative classrooms 123
   and co-operative learning 58–61
   as a social event 1
   making the 'what' and 'how' explicit 123
   maximising learning 124
literature roulette 72–4
Lyn Thompson's classroom community 10

metacognitive language for literacy 58–9
modelling
   collaborative composition 112
   genres 101
   keeping a reading log 81
   roles for role reading 86
   successful behaviours 32
   thinking 95
   see also explicit teaching

paired reading 70–1
parent response journals 89
participation 59–60
partner reading 28, 35, 67–70
peer support for writing 93–4
peer evaluation of writing 117–21
persuasive writing 106–9
persuasive writing sheet 108
piggybacking 56, 76
positive interdependence 50–2
   structuring for 52–58
posters 105–6
predictagloss 83–4
proactive response to change 125–6
process of writing 110, 112
punctuation 110, 111, 112
put-downs 42
pyramiding 54

random grouping 53
range sheets, reading 65
range sheets, writing 91, 95–7
raps and rhymes 31–2, 65, 110
readers theatre 67
reading
   extending responses 72–82
   practice 67–72
   strategies 83–6
reading aloud to the class 32, 66, 97–100
reading logs 81–2
reading records 89
reciprocal teaching 86

redlight-greenlight thinking 54–5
responding to change 125–6
responsibility 38–9
reward (recognition) interdependence 51
role charts 14
role reading 86–7
roles
   for class meetings 7, 9, 15
   for revising the rules for arguments 108
roundtable 56
RRRR (reflect, read, record, respond) 84–5

school literacy communities 22–28, 126–7
self-evaluation circles 36
self-evaluation of writing 117–21
shared experiences 31–2
sharing circles 31, 95
   feedback on writing 118–9
sharing information through print 22–28
sharing text 62–3
silent reading 28
six hats 55
spelling 110, 112
spoken language 59
standard English 110
strategies
   for creating reading/writing communities 10–28
   for writing 93–121
   for writing effectively 114–17
structuring
   for co-operation 9–10
   for co-operative learning 49–58
   for co-operative writing 113–14
   for positive interdependence 52–8
   for using print 8–9

success, children's experience of 41
successful behaviours 33–4, 35
   partner reading 68, 69

T charts 14, 15, 17
teacher responses to individual writing 113
teacher think alouds 111
teacher's role 122
teaching communities 127
teaching reading, goals and strategies 63–90
think/pair/share 53, 59–60, 95, 108
think/pair/four/share 53–4
three-step interviews 54
three-step process for successful behaviours 35
trust blocks 36
trust 39–31
TV guides 101–2
TV reviews 102

whip 56
writing
   demonstrations 118
   evaluation 117–21
   peer support 93–4
   process and conventions 110–14
writing checkers 104
writing contracts 120–1
writing effectively 114–17
writing forms (genres) 91, 95–7
writing practice 102–3
writing program, goals 92–4

Y charts 11–12
   co-operative behaviours 46–7
   on harassment 11–12
   on a person 12
   partner reading 68
   purposes 11

RESOURCES FOR CO-OPERATIVE LEARNING FROM ELEANOR CURTAIN PUBLISHING

Games That Work
Co-operative Games and Activities for the Primary School Classroom
Susan Hill

This book is a 'how to' manual presenting games and activities which engage children and introduce them to the idea and the practice of collaboration. It focuses on communication and co-operation, the underpinning of all learning.

The underlying structures are carefully planned so that the features of collaboration are made explicit and the games are presented not as isolated activities, but as preparation and structuring for group work.

The book presents the following topics and activities:

Introduction: How we learn co-operatively
- Elements of co-operative learning: shared goals; positive interdependence; individual responsibility; teaching co-operative skills; giving specific feedback.

Co-operative games and activities
- Forming group games: getting acquainted; mixing it up; pairs and partners; making space for people; communication games and activities.
- Working as a group: games, activities, roles.
- Games and activities for problem solving: projects.
- Games and activities for managing differences; consensus game and activities.
- Games for big spaces.

ISBN 1 87532 716 9 illustrated 128 pages

The Collaborative Classroom
A guide to co-operative learning
Susan and Tim Hill

The Collaborative Classroom is a creative and practial guide for teachers on implementing and gaining maximum benefit for students from co-operative learning.

The book focuses and identifies the areas where co-operative skills are needed: forming groups — working as a group, problem solving as a group; and managing differences — discusssing problems, offering suggestions and providing practical applications.

The Collaborative Classroom is both practical and enccuraging and includes dozens of activities to get the beginning teacher started.

ISBN 1 875327 00 2 illustrated 162 pp

I Teach
A Guide to Inspiring Classroom Leadership
Joan Dalton and Julie Boyd

A professional development book providing specific and practical insights into the 'what' and 'how' of effective learning and teaching.

The ideas are presented succinctly and visually.

- About teaching and leadership: what are your goals, what are you working towards?
- Walk the leader's walk: as a teacher you are a leader and need to be aware of your leadership role and skills.
- Building relationships with others: insights into personal relationship building.
- Creating a community of learners: the key ingredients for balancing individuality and collaboration.
- Empowering growth in others: a focus on effective thinking, metacognition and meta-learning principles.
- Working of self-growth: modelling the principles of both personal and professional growth.
- On reflection: identifying personal strengths, highlighting areas for self-improvement, and planning for balanced leadership.

ISBN 1 87532 711 8 illustrated 128 pages

Becoming Responsible Learners
Stragtegies for positive classroom management
Joan Dalton and Mark Collis

An extremely practical and highly readable book on strategies and guide-lines for classroom management this book is the result of observing effective collaborative teachers at work and talking to them about their beliefs and classroom practices.

It is an invaluable asset to teachers who want to encourage children to take responsibility for their own learning and behaviour.
ISBN 1 875327 05 3 illustrated 80 pp

Readers Theatre
Performing the text
Susan Hill

Readers Theatre is a simple, informal and motivating way to involve students in the study of literature by group story-telling, shared reading, improvisation and performance of a favourite story.

Readers Theatre provides complete scripts for performance, guide-lines for helping children write their own scripts, aids and ideas for improvisation and lists of texts that work well in adaptation.
ISBN 1 875327 01 0 illustrated 88 pp

Raps & Rhymes & Maths
Compiled by Ann and Johnny Baker

A collection of traditional and modern rhymes, riddles and stories with mathematical themes, Raps & Rhymes & Maths can be used to provide a welcome break from more formal activities or can form the introduction or conclusion of a maths lesson.

The raps, rhymes and stories provide openings for mathematical investigations and, most importantly, provide a source of enjoyment.
ISBN 1 875327 07 X illustrated 90 pp

Raps & Rhymes
Selected by Susan Hill

Raps & Rhymes is a stimulating selection of traditional chants and rhymes that have been played with, improvised on and read by children of all ages. Reading aloud as a group, joining in a chant or a rhyme is a great warm-up to any lesson, and an effective way to build up a feeling of cohesiveness in class.

Susan Hill, Senior Lecturer in Curriculum Studies at the South Australian College of Advanced Education, has chosen pieces for Improvising, Clapping and Clicking, Action Rhymes, Part-reading and just plain Nonsense.
ISBN 1 875327 03 7 illustrated 80 pp

For information on these and other titles contact
Eleanor Curtain Publishing
906 Malvern Road Armadale 3143
Tel (03) 822 0344   Fax (03) 824 8851

Distributed in New Zealand by
Ashton Scolastic
165 Marua Road, Panmure, New Zealand
Tel (09) 579 6089   Fax (09) 579 3860